Routledge Revivals

Economic and Monetary Union in Europe

In its pursuit of economic integration, economic and monetary union (EMU) had become a primary commitment for the European Community. Originally published in 1974, this study sets out to examine the meaning of economic union and its relationship with monetary union.

The contributors look at the problems and costs for attaining economic union for the member states of the EEC at the time. Steven Robson writes on economic management. Paul Woolley examines the integration of capital markets. Santosh Mukherjee looks at the implications of labour market policy. Geoffrey Denton and Adam Ridley consider the impact of economic and monetary union on regional problems. Alan Prest is concerned with tax harmonisation specifically Value Added Tax and Corporation Tax and Douglas Dosser discusses the development of a European Community budget.

Though the long-term benefits of EMU were clear, in the short term it would impose strains and pressures on national economies and particular sectors within them. This study goes a long way to clarifying where these difficulties would arise and suggests some ways of coping with them.

Economic and Monetary Union in Europe

Edited by
Geoffrey Denton

Routledge
Taylor & Francis Group

First published in 1974
by Croom Helm

This edition first published in 2022 by Routledge
2 Park Square, Milton Park, Abingdon, Oxon, OX14 4RN

and by Routledge
605 Third Avenue, New York, NY 10017

Routledge is an imprint of the Taylor & Francis Group, an informa business

© 1974 The Federal Trust

Publisher's Note
The publisher has gone to great lengths to ensure the quality of this reprint but points out that some imperfections in the original copies may be apparent.

Disclaimer
The publisher has made every effort to trace copyright holders and welcomes correspondence from those they have been unable to contact.

A Library of Congress record exists under ISBN: 0856641367

ISBN: 978-1-032-19589-6 (hbk)
ISBN: 978-1-003-25994-7 (ebk)
ISBN: 978-1-032-19593-3 (pbk)

Book DOI 10.4324/9781003259947

ECONOMIC AND MONETARY UNION IN EUROPE

Edited by Geoffrey Denton

CROOM HELM LONDON

First published 1974
℗ 1974 The Federal Trust
Croom Helm Ltd 2-10 St. John's Road, London SW11
in association with
The Federal Trust for Education and Research
12A Maddox Street, London W1

ISBN 0-85664-136-7

Printed by Biddles of Guildford

Contents

PREFACE

This book results from the work of a Federal Trust Study Group
established in November 1972 to examine the economic implications of
plans to establish a monetary union of the EEC countries.

The Chairman of the Group was John Pinder, Director of Political
and Economic Planning, and Professor Douglas Dosser of the University
of York acted as Rapporteur. Thanks are due to them for stimulating
the writing of the papers, ensuring that they benefitted from lively
discussion and comment, and for summarising the work of the Group in
a short report, *Economic Union in the EEC,* published in July 1974.

The Federal Trust also wishes to thank the other members of the
Group for advising and commenting on the papers: Mr. L. Airey,
Mr. G.R. Denton, Dr. T. Josling, Professor J.E. Meade, Professor A.R.
Prest, Mr. A. Ridley, Mr. S. Robson, Mr. B. Tarleton, Mr. P.K.
Woolley, Mr. M. Zinkin and Mr. J. Dodsworth.

Among the wider number of participants in the Elvetham Hall
conference, the Federal Trust is particularly grateful to Sir Alec
Cairncross, who took the chair in the opening session, to Professor
Theo Peeters of the University of Louvain for summing up, and to
several senior British and European Commission officials who took an
active part in the discussions. Thanks are due also to Penny David and
Nicole Laplagne of the Federal Trust for organising the Group; to
Diarmid McLaughlin of the European Community Institute for
University Studies for initiating the work of the British and other
national groups; to Political and Economic Planning, who provided
facilities for meetings; and to the S.S.R.C. Public Sector Studies
Programme of the University of York, whose members provided
some analysis and statistics.

The papers presented as chapters in this book remain, of course, the
personal responsibility of the authors. In particular, even in the cases
where the authors are or were holding official posts, the chapters
represent only their personal views.

1 THE MEANING OF ECONOMIC UNION

Geoffrey Denton

Recent studies of the prospects for European economic integration in the 1970s and 1980s have emphasised monetary union. The purpose of the present Federal Trust study is to examine the meaning of economic union. Subsequent chapters examine this phenomenon from the various standpoints of stabilisation policy, capital markets, regional problems and policy, fiscal policy, and the Community budget. The purpose of the present chapter is to introduce the papers on these different aspects by some general remarks about the meaning of economic union, the relationship between it and monetary union, the distinction between the final condition of full economic and monetary union (hereafter called EMU) and the transitional phase leading up to it, and the relationship between the policy-created EMU and the process of autonomous integration.

The Aims of Economic Union

The group spent some time in its early meetings in attempts to define what it considered to be the aims of economic union. It recognised the diversity of views which must exist on the meaning of so general a concept. Nevertheless it was able to arrive at a working description to guide its further work.

The first matter to clarify is the distinction between economic and political objectives. The primary aim of economic union for some people may be to contribute to the creation of a political union, which in turn is desired for internal and external political and strategic reasons: the avoidance of conflict among west European nations, or the strengthening of western Europe *vis à vis* other powers. This group was not directly concerned with such broad political motivations, but rather with elucidating the economic benefits and costs of economic union.

Economic union may be regarded as desirable in its own right if it can be shown to contribute to the economic welfare of the people of western Europe. This overall welfare criterion can be disaggregated to describe the normal set of national economic objectives: growth of overall output per head, efficient allocation and use of resources,

1

stabilisation of the levels of activity, employment and income, an acceptable distribution of income, regional balance, and preservation of the physical and social environments. Some of these objectives may be controversial; for example, not everyone would agree that regional balance is a proper objective even for national governments, and many might hesitate to propose it as an objective of the Community to be given similar status to that which it is accorded in the existing nations. Simply to list the objectives is in any event rather meaningless; more important is the ordering of priorities among them and defining the trade-offs that are to be accepted when they are in conflict. These are matters of much political debate in the individual countries; it follows that they must also be controversial for the Community as a whole. An ordered set of economic objectives for any society also requires that it has adequate political institutions to determine them. Since such institutions have yet to be created at European level, it follows that there is considerable difficulty in arriving at a set of aims of a European economic union.

The definition of economic union in the context of the European Community is thus extremely difficult. We have, therefore, in this book, preferred to let the definition emerge from the detailed accounts of problems and policies in specific areas. This does not detract from the validity of the study of European economic union, any more than the similar problems involved in defining economic union at the level of the nation state imply that one should be inhibited from studying its economic problems.

A fruitful approach to the definition of economic union at the European level is to attempt to clarify the special characteristics of an economic union in western Europe that would enable it to make specific contributions to the general set of Community/national objectives. In this way one can set out a number of intermediate objectives of forming an economic union that would contribute to the ultimate aims. These would include: the creation of a larger market free of distortions, and enabling economic gains through specialisation in production and wider choice in consumption; stabilisation of the internal conditions of this larger market through joint economic management and policy co-ordination; stabilisation of the external conditions through a common commercial policy, external monetary policy, etc. The difficulty of this approach is that these intermediate objectives have all been considered in various ways also to bring disadvantages to the member states, and it is therefore necessary to find the balance of benefits and costs of the policy communalisation and co-ordination involved in economic union before one can reasonably judge whether it is beneficial for any one member. The subsequent chapters of this book make no attempt to hide the costs, which arise for some members on some policies, and indeed much of the discussion is concerned with setting out the safeguards, the positive policies and in general the conditions in which the members of an economic union could be reasonably reassured that costs and benefits would be fairly distributed and that net gains would result for each and every one.

The Relation between Economic Union and Monetary Union

Economic union is often regarded in current discussions as necessary to the achievement of monetary union. Thus many of the elements of economic union: common regional policy, fiscal harmonisation, a common budget, can be treated simply as conditions for the successful adoption and operation of a monetary union. But to be content with this would be to let the monetary tail wag the economic dog with a vengeance. Economic union as a requirement for monetary union can only be accepted if the case for monetary union can itself be firmly based on theory and empirical evidence. This has been the subject of many official and private reports and studies, including an earlier Federal Trust Report.[1] It is not necessary here to do more than outline the kind of case that can be made, and no attempt is made to argue its validity.

The main elements of the case are as follows:
(1)　that Europe is, or will soon become, an optimal currency area: with much greater internal than external trade and other economic interdependence, as measured for example by proportions of GNP traded internally and externally, internal factor movements, equalisation of prices;
(2)　that the individual capital markets in western Europe are too small to support stable individual currencies, and that price, wage and other interdependences are so great that parity changes do not function to restore payments equilibrium;
(3)　that European industry requires to be organised on a continental scale in order to retain the power to compete with the US, Japan, USSR. (This argument requires that the option of organisation in interdependence with US industry is ruled out for political or economic motives.)

The evidence on these issues is strong but not overwhelming. Benelux countries have a very high degree of dependence on trade within the EEC, but Germany, France and Italy only moderate, and the UK still very small though likely to grow rapidly. Eire has a high degree of interdependence, but this is primarily dependence on the UK. Cross-frontier capital investments have come predominantly from the US, and labour movements predominantly from non-EEC southern Europe.

The evidence of the inadequate size of European capital markets and national currency reserves is strong, but the evidence on prices does not support the interdependence hypothesis. Price trends have in practice diverged, and the parity adjustments, at least up to the period of monetary turbulence since 1971, have been fairly well correlated with the relative price trends over long periods, whereas the argument requires parity changes to be rapidly offset by relative price adjustments. Micro-economic studies also show little tendency towards price equalisation among the Six. Moreover, the inadequacy of reserves to take the strain of speculative movements can support an argument for flexible parities as well as one for monetary union if prices are not interdependent. Willingness to adjust the peg in response to long-term disequilibria, and to allow fluctuations within a broad band to meet short-term changes, could then alleviate the capital market problem.

The argument from interdependence is certainly strengthened if one examines *trends* rather than actualities, as has already been noted in the case of UK dependence on intra-trade. Moreover, interdependence to some extent constitutes a self-fulfilling prophecy. The problem is to judge the moment, if any, at which the economies are about to become sufficiently interdependent to justify a monetary union.

The Transition to Economic Union

Even if it is judged that interdependence is already so advanced that an early creation of a monetary union is necessary in the 1970s, there remains the problem of the transitional period. Agreement on the creation of a monetary union does not necessarily justify policies during the transitional period that will be appropriate only in the conditions of fuller interdependence brought about, in part, by the final union. There is a political case in favour of 'crisis therapy'; the early creation of an 'unbalanced' union in which monetary integration has far outrun the harmonisation of economic policies, on the ground that it is necessary to create problems by committing ourselves to immediate monetary integration, since only in attempting to solve these problems will national governments create the necessary common institutions and the common policies. But this argument is unconvincing politically as well as economically harmful; it is just as probable that the shock of a ruthless adoption of this 'monetarist' strategy would disrupt the whole process of monetary and economic integration by causing one or more countries to leave the Community.

Being primarily concerned with the requirements of economic union, the group adopted the working assumption of eventual monetary integration. However, they took the view that permanent locking of the internal parities of the member countries was not to be expected in the near future. The freedom to adjust exchange parities was required in order to deal with the problems of price-cost adjustment, until such time as autonomous integration had removed the existing divergencies in trends of relative factor prices and productivity levels in different member countries. The group acknowledged that speculative currency flows into and out of various national currencies might result in parity adjustments which had no real economic rationale. However, while this strengthened the case for an early fixing of rates, it certainly did not make an early fixing of rates feasible in advance of adequate mutual support operations to prevent parities being upset by such movements.

Although the group had been mainly concerned to discuss policy at national and European levels, the members were always aware that the really important question is to what extent integration is in practice taking place among firms, banks, trade unions, etc. within the European Community, and the effects on the main economic variables, prices, wages, etc. Unfortunately, there is little firm evidence of the extent of this increasing integration to which policy must be adapted, and more analysis of the extent and of the probable future development of this 'autonomous' integration is urgent. Much of the case for monetary union, and therefore for the concomitant economic policies discussed in this report, hinges on the actuality and the prospects of the real process of integration.

A Summary of the Findings

The conclusions arrived at by the group have already been published in a summary Report, prepared by the Chairman and Rapporteur. It may, nevertheless, be helpful to set out very briefly at this point the main conclusions of the group. Some of these relate to matters such as industrial policy and social policy which are not treated in separate chapters below; most are derived from these chapters.

The group considered the impact of monetary integration on the business cycles within the Community. They concluded that present analysis of evidence does not promote a clear judgement as to how far the business cycles will be unified, nor whether such unification of fluctuations would have the consequences of amplifying or dampening the overall movements. Further analysis of this problem is urgently required. Concerning the problem of assigning instruments to Community and national institutions, there was a general presumption in favour of assigning monetary instruments to the Community and fiscal instruments to the national administrations, if only on the ground of administrative simplicity. However, it was recognised that, given the development of fiscal powers at Community level, there would be a substantial case for some mix of monetary and fiscal policies at this level for the purpose of controlling the Community cycle. Further, since the Community cycle would be influenced by the autonomous actions of member states, there would also be a need for some Community supervision and control of national policies in respect of budget deficits, prices and incomes policies, etc. It was also noted that the consequences of Community action to stabilise the European economy would be unevenly spread over the various national and sub-national regions and that this would require some degree of differentiation in the application of stabilisation policies. Since fiscal policies are more readily differentiable than monetary policies in a monetary union, this was an additional argument for the existence of fiscal stabilisation instruments at Community level.

The group considered the implications for factor markets of monetary integration. They concluded that there was no need for an early and complete liberalisation of capital movements. It might continue to be desirable, especially in the light of particular problems in member countries and in some of the regions, that there should be controls on the free movement of capital toward one part of the Community and from another. There could be no general presumption that the gains from freer movement of capital would outweigh the costs. Given some increased liberalisation of capital movements internally, it would be essential to set up a common ring-fence of external capital controls. Massive movement of labour from one country to another was not expected, but there would be a problem of redundancy as industry was restructured in the face of competition unrestrained by any parity adjustments. This redundancy would create regional problems where industries affected were concentrated in particular regions.

The group noted that the removal of the instrument of parity adjustment could result in a worsening of the competitive situation of some regions. This effect would be in addition to the effect of the customs union in making some regions more peripheral, and therefore more disadvantaged, than they had been within their national markets. It followed that there would be a need for two kinds of regional policy to exist in the monetary union. First, national governments would have to be permitted to continue, and possibly even to develop further, their existing regional policies. It was recognised that these could create problems for competition policy, and that criteria, preferably of a very simple kind, would have to be agreed for defining the existence of a regional problem which would justify such national policies. Secondly, there would be a need for a substantial Community regional fund to enable some substantial redistribution of the gains from integration towards those regions which suffered as a consequence. In order that the transfers should be significant, there were two requirements in the operation of this fund. First, it should be large enough to generate substantial transfers; and secondly, the regions eligible for assistance would have to be selectively chosen; that is, it would not be meaningful if each country's own definition of its problem areas were to be accepted without any reference to Community-wide criteria. The group further considered, however, that aid to particular regions from the Community fund would probably be most efficient if granted in support of national programmes for the development of particular regions rather than existing alongside national programmes.

The discussion of industrial policy in the Community has been prolonged but not very productive of results, even in terms of policy. The group felt that the development of industrial policy in the Community would be facilitated by an economic and monetary union. They wished to draw attention to the need to make industrial policy, both at national and at Community level, more coherent than it has been. In particular, it was necessary to resolve some of the contradictions, for example, as between merger policy and competition policy It was also necessary in view of the wide range of proposals already under discussion, to concentrate on a few priority areas in which progress towards a common policy could most easily be achieved.

The possible increase in redundancy would require the establishment of a common fund in order to share the burden equitably within the Community. Regarding social security in general, the group thought that alignment both of contributions and of benefits was likely to be a slow process, dependent on progress in other aspects of redistribution within the Community There was a case for alignment of contributions on the ground of creating fair conditions for competition, but this could not be pressed while the burdens of standardisation would be excessive for low-income member countries. Equalisation of benefits would have to await development of the Community spirit. The group also concluded that a European economic union could make a contribution to social innovation, and that this indeed would be an important means of making the economic union acceptable to public opinion. In particular, common policies towards problems such as the environment, participation in industry, the quality of life, etc. could be facilitated since the Community could modify, so far as internal trade was concerned at least, the competitive pressures which tend to bring about the neglect of these social problems.

It was accepted that, following the present development of common fiscal policy, the Value Added Tax (VAT) must be assumed to be the major basis for the future Community budget. However, in the light of the discussion of national and regional problems arising in a monetary union, there was a need to reconsider the approach to the harmonisation of taxation. Possibly the VAT should not be equalised for all member states, since differentiation of the VAT (without border tax adjustments being made) would be a powerful instrument for solving regional problems. It was likely that the VAT would develop into effectively a two-tier tax, with part of the revenues going to national governments and another part to the Community. Discrimination in the rates of VAT could be exercised at both levels. Discrimination at the Community level would be the most significant since this would enable effective transfers from one member state to another. Although VAT was currently the basis of discussion, the group also considered the possible advantages of a future Community Corporation Tax as a major source of Community finance. Such a common tax would have substantial advantages in removing barriers to the development of industry across the frontiers, and it was possible that national and regional discrimination in fiscal policy could more easily be engineered out of such a tax than out of the common VAT.

The development of common policies already foreseen in these conclusions would require a substantial development of the Community's budget. In the absence of any very clear forecasts about precisely which policies would be adopted, and the size of the expenditure that they would generate, the group were unable to make much progress in forecasting the expenditure requirements of the Community. Even on the revenue side, it was difficult to make any firm forecasts, but following the existing decisions about the Community's budgetary resources, and on the basis of certain assumptions about the percentage of certain taxes that would be available to the Community, it was possible to arrive at conditional estimates of the potential size of the Community's revenue. The revenue available could then be allocated according to the priorities given to the various expenditures. It was noted that the larger the Community budget in general, the greater the potential for a true Community spirit in finding solutions to economic and social problems. It was also essential, however, if this Community spirit were to be achieved, that national members should not necessarily expect to receive back in expenditures everything they contributed in revenues.

References

1. *European Monetary Integration,* Federal Trust, London, 1972 (the Magnifico-Williamson Report).

2 ECONOMIC MANAGEMENT IN A MONETARY UNION

Steven Robson

At the Hague Summit in 1969, the Six agreed to create an economic and monetary union. The subsequent Werner Report became the blueprint for EMU, but was never embodied in a Council Resolution and therefore remains a background document. There are two EMU resolutions. The first of March 1971, followed the Werner Report in many respects. It stated that the aim was to turn the Community into an area "in which persons, goods, services and capital move freely and without distortions of competition, but without thereby giving rise to structural or regional imbalances, and under conditions enabling business to expand their activities on a Community scale'. At the same time the Community woul form a 'separate monetary entity' in the international monetary system.

The principal features of EMU as described in the resolution are: complete and irreversible convertibility of currencies, elimination of margins of fluctuation and irrevocably fixed exchange rates; a Community organisation of Central Banks; transfer to the Community level of 'the requisite decisions on economic policy' and the power and responsibility 'necessary for the cohesion of the union and the effectiveness of Community action' in the fields of:
 (1)   internal monetary and credit policies;
 (2)   monetary policy with the rest of the world;
 (3)   policies relating to the capital market and to movements of capital to and from the rest of the world;
 (4)   budgetary and fiscal policies (in particular the variation in 'the essential elements' of public budgets and the size, the use and the methods of financing of the budget balance);
 (5)   the regional and structural measures necessary to the balanced development of the Community.

The first stage in the process of forming the union was to last three years, finishing at the end of 1973, but the resolution was rather vague about its contents. It merely stated that these 'should include' a strengthening of the consultation procedures, particularly prior consultations, and the introduction of a system whereby the Council would lay down the broad outlines of economic policy at the Community level and also quantitative guidelines for the 'essential elements' of national budgets. Similar provisions were made for consultation and guidelines on monetary and credit policies.

The second resolution, of 21 March 1972, stated that a member state which was planning measures which differed from the Council guidelines should consult, if necessary within the Council, before adopting such measures. To facilitate such consultations the resolution made provision for a High Level Steering Group.

Progress in Stage 1

It could be claimed that these resolutions were reasonably fully implemented. Such a claim would have to rely somewhat on the rather vague drafting of the resolutions, and on the fact that the prior consultations procedure was never really put to the test, but in each area there now exists a Community body which can be seen as fulfilling the letter, if not the spirit, of the resolutions. During Stage 1 the Council of Ministers met three times a year to discuss the economic situation. At the first meeting developments in the previous year were reviewed. The second concentrated on prospects for the current year and decreed economic guidelines for the Community. In practice the guidelines were, however, expressed in very general terms and more concerned with ends than means. The third meeting of the Council approved the Annual Report on the Economic Situation in the Community which was then sent to national parliaments for their information and consideration. This Annual Report reviewed the problems and objectives of economic policy in the member states and set out the main policy guidelines for the year ahead.

In Stage 1 these discussions were essentially consultative. Although the member states tended to share common objectives and, very often, common problems, the particular circumstances which they faced varied considerably so that policies appropriate to one country were unlikely to be right for all. For this reason, the guidelines set out in the Annual Report and promulgated by the Council made no attempt to suggest standard economic policy measures which all members should adopt. Rather they indicated the broad lines of macro-economic policy which the Council considered appropriate to each country if it was to maintain consistency with the policies of other members and to have the best chance of promoting the objectives they held in common.

The Community had also established a series of more specific committees which met regularly at the official level. Their names are reasonably self-explanatory: the Monetary Policy, Conjunctural Policy, Budgetary Policy and Medium-term Policy Committees. In addition, a Committee of Central Bank Governors and, as already mentioned, a High Level Steering Group were set up. These committees, in some cases with supporting sub-committees, provided a forum for a continuous exchange of information about economic developments, policies and prospects in member states. As appropriate, they also assisted in the process of agreeing a common approach for the Community in international discussions, for example, on international monetary reform. Finally, they also carried out *ad hoc* instructions from the Council of which the periodic anti-inflation exercises are a good example.

There was a considerable amount of disappointment in the Community about the outcome of Stage I. This usually focused on the fact that several currencies were outside the Community 'snake' set up under the 1972 resolution, but really extended over the whole area of economic co-ordination and consultation. Basically, while the Brussels machinery was used for the exchange of information, there was very little in the way of common determination of economic and monetary policies.

The reasons are not hard to find: Member states do not always have the same problems; one country can have excess demand while others have excess capacity. Even when they have similar problems, they often have different priorities, for example, between inflation and unemployment. They have different ways of tackling a given problem; for example, the Continentals tend to rely on monetary and budgetary policy rather than incomes policy to tackle inflation. During Stage I they could indulge their differences, since there was often little or no need for a common approach; economic interdependence was not so great that a failure to have a common approach throughout the Community led to significant economic instability. This is not to deny that there were sub-areas within the Community where a common approach was valuable.

Over time the costs of failing to consult and co-ordinate will become greater and national governments are going to have to face the problem that it is likely to become increasingly impossible to manage their economies in isolation. This is saying no more than that increased interdependence among the economies of the Nine will mean that each member's domestic policy will have an increasing impact on the economies of other members.

Shaw[1] has outlined in some detail the consequences of forming an economic union for national stabilisation policies. He emphasised the increase in the marginal propensity to import which could be expected and which, while making autonomous shocks to national economies less de-stabilising, would make national economies more sensitive to income changes emanating from other member states and render national stabilisation policies less effective. At the same time, trade diversion from third countries would make the union as a whole more stable.

This suggests that increased and more detailed consultation will become necessary and desirable before national governments take or implement domestic economic policy decisions. A lack of such consultation would eventually lead to a situation in which national governments take policy decisions in isolation which lead to undesirable effects in other member states. These, in turn, take offsetting action so reducing the effectiveness of the original policy. Rapid changes in the economic climate of the Community which would follow isolated and competitive demand management of this sort would be in no member's interests. Therefore there will come a stage when entry into closer and more detailed discussions of domestic economic policies and objectives will bring the benefit of reducing the likelihood of an unstable economic environment.

It is not easy to forecast when this gain becomes significant. There are certain forms of interdependence, such as trade and factor mobility, which can be measured, at least in principle, but there are also less tangible aspects relating, for example, to institutions, tastes and aspirations. Even if it were possible to express interdependence quantitatively there would remain the problem of establishing any clear relationship between the degree of interdependence and the need for economic co-ordination. It may be possible to explore some aspects of interdependence with economic models, and possibly this is work that the proposed European Institute for Economic Analysis and Research could usefully do. However, the nature of the problem probably precludes any clear-cut *ex ante* answers.

It would, of course, be undesirable to wait until the effects of interdependence become apparent *ex post*. Consequently the best course is to develop the consultations and co-ordination procedure in a way that will eventually permit the Community economy to be managed centrally by Community institutions. This development must take place in a manner that enables the Community to meet whatever need for co-ordination emerges along the way. As the need will always be uncertain, there is something to be said for expecting it to be greater rather than smaller, although this will make it difficult to justify to domestic opinion the extent of co-ordination at any moment in time.

Stage II

One approach to Stage II would have been to tackle the weakness of the present economic co-ordination procedure, the lack of a common analytical base, and the lack of a sense of purpose.

First, the analytical base. The representatives of each member state presumably know a good deal about the likely development of their national economy but less about that of their partners. This must make it difficult to discuss in much depth the guidelines for national policies. The analytical base could be improved by the development of the Community forecasting procedures. In the first place the Community could prepare annually five-year medium-term economic projections for the Community and its component parts. Secondly, short-term, say two- or three-year, forecasts should be prepared at least twice a year. Both the short- and the medium-term work would probably be best done in a semi-autonomous body like the proposed European Institute for Economic Analysis and Research. These forecasts could be laid before the Council of Ministers together with related Commission economic policy proposals. The medium-term forecasts would be used to establish medium-term objectives, particularly for national and Community public expenditure and for structural policies. The short-term guidelines would keep both the national economy and the Community as a whole moving towards the medium-term objectives.

At the same time it would be necessary to have a continuous system of monitoring the national economies. This would enable the Community to ensure that the agreed policy guidelines were being implemented and that these were having the desired effects. Any serious departure from guidelines would trigger consultations, as would the movement of key indicators away from their expected path. In these consultations a member state, or states, would have to justify any change of policy to the rest of the Community and the Council would be able to make specific policy recommendations to the member states. If it were felt that any member state was not playing a full part in this process the Community could impose economic sanctions on it. For example, the member's access to Community credit facilities might be restricted for a time or, if some pooling of reserves had also occurred as part of Stage II, the rate of interest paid on its balances held with the European Monetary Co-operation Fund might be reduced.

This system of sanctions would be intended to meet the second shortcoming, the lack of sense of purpose. The immediate purpose would be to avoid the sanction. Member states would submit to this discipline to avoid a situation arising in the future in which the degree of co-ordination failed to match the needs of the time. In addition Stage II could also have been devoted to some nitty-gritty work such as the harmonisation of 'planning procedures'. This can be taken to cover national plans, where they exist, as well as more restricted systems of management and control such as that underlying the UK's annual White Paper on Public Expenditure. Harmonisation would involve establishing common timetables, time horizons, coverage and methodology. Although work of this sort would have little public appeal, it has to be done if economic co-ordination is to operate smoothly.

Beyond Stage II

Planning further progress towards EMU requires careful thought to be given to the form and functioning of full union and also to the most appropriate path towards that union. This is another example of the sort of work the Community might undertake during Stage II.

It has sometimes been argued that progress towards monetary union could act as a spur to economic convergence and eventual union. The Werner Report, with its uncritical emphasis on a common currency, tended to encourage such thinking and the EMU resolutions of 1971 and 1972 were certainly biased in the monetary direction. This approach always lacked intellectual conviction and the experience of Stage I has caused it to be questioned even by its erstwhile proponents. Four of the Community currencies are floating outside the 'snake' and even currencies within the snake have been subject to fairly frequent changes of value and to recurrent speculative pressure. In part these difficulties have reflected the changed international monetary environment. There is now a greater readiness to make exchange rate changes than at the time the Werner Report was written and, in addition, there is a much greater volume of internationally mobile funds ready to move in and out of currencies in anticipation of changes in rates. It is possible that reform of the international monetary system may reduce some of the present instability in monetary arrangements and enable the snake to function with fewer stresses. But even if this does happen, the snake itself will have limited value. It is sometimes claimed, especially by the French, that the existence of the snake encourages the harmonisation of economic policies. It is hard either to prove or to disprove such a claim, but there is no reason why the snake should have this effect as long as member states are prepared to alter exchange rates within the snake or, in the final assessment, float out of it. The Paris Summit emphasised that 'fixed but adjustable' parities were the 'essential' basis for achieving EMU and this reduces greatly the need to harmonise policies.

Monetary union is, of course, much more than the snake. It means the irreversible locking of currencies at fixed and unchangeable parities and the absence of any margins of fluctuation. This could have a great impact on national economies since it would remove one of the main instruments of national economic policy.

At present if, for example, a relatively rapid rise in UK costs and prices makes UK output uncompetitive, the UK authorities are able to alter the sterling exchange rate to restore equilibrium. However, if UK prices rose relatively quickly in a monetary union with locked exchange rates, the UK would be unable to take the necessary action. As a result output in the UK would fall and unemployment would rise. At the same time demand would increase for the output from those parts of the

14

union where prices had risen relatively slowly and would lead to bottlenecks, shortages and demand inflation. Such national effort as could be made to correct these tendencies would in each case exacerbate the problems of member states at the opposite extreme; thus reflation in 'high price' areas would add to demand and inflationary pressures in 'low price' ones and demand restraints in 'low price' areas would aggravate unemployment elsewhere.

It has been suggested that as part of a full EMU, the free flow of capital and labour would counter-balance these tendencies. This is most unlikely. The post-war experience of many individual countries has shown that these market forces do not solve regional problems. If anything market forces tend to exacerbate regional imbalances by attracting capital to areas of high economic activity. As a result governments have found it necessary to intervene to try and solve these problems. However, despite the inducements they have offered, there has been insufficient mobility of labour and capital to eliminate the problems. In principle such disparities could be countered by resource transfers from the fully employed and expanding parts of the union to those suffering from unemployment and stagnation. Such transfers presently take place within the UK in favour of areas like Scotland and Northern Ireland. But if the differences in economic performance between the member states remained much the same as at present, the size of these transfers would have to be truly massive, far beyond anything so far contemplated for the regional development fund.[2]

It is at present difficult to imagine that the political will exists, or in the foreseeable future will exist, to institute such a system within the Community. Consequently monetary union must await a high degree of convergence in the performance of nationa economies. Unfortunately there seems little that can be done to bring about such convergence. UK governments have for years tried, with little success, to bring the UK performance closer to that of, say, Germany. It seems possible that increased interdependence in the EEC and increased familiarity with techniques, organisation, tastes and attitudes in other countries may gradually bring about convergence, but it will be a long haul.

In these circumstances the EEC might decide to settle for a less extensive form of EMU in 1980 than that outlined in the 1971 resolution. This could include: all national currencies linked by some arrangement along the lines of the 'snake', but with rates adjustable after consultation; the European Monetary Co-operation Fund (EMCF) responsible for maintaining the margins of fluctuation of currencies and able to provide some credit, with Community supervision; closer consultation on national measures affecting the Community and other member states, possibly backed up by economic sanctions; the introduction of Community structural policies such as a significant regional development fund.

National Economic Management

National economic management could be greatly affected by progress towards EMU, and this raises the question of developing Community instruments of economic management. Economic management is, of course, a very sensitive area politically, often taken to be a major reason for electoral defeat or victory. Consequently the political obstacles to centralisation of this responsibility in Brussels must not be underestimated. At the national level the major purposes of economic policy, and particularly budgetary policy, are often described as income distribution, demand management and resource allocation, especially allocation between the public and private sectors. While the instruments used are not specific to any one of these areas, this provides a useful framework for examining the implications of EMU.

At the moment the Community's approach to centralised economic management is virtually non-existent. The Community budget is equivalent to about 0.67 per cent of Community GNP, and on present policies is unlikely to expand to much more than 1 per cent. By comparison the national budgets of the Nine are equivalent to about 20-30 per cent of national GNPs.

However, the Community's moves towards fiscal harmonisation have important implications for national economic management. The Community has approached fiscal harmonisation largely with the objective of abolishing 'fiscal frontiers' and securing the free movement of goods and services. Directives have been prepared on the harmonisation of the structure of VAT, comparing taxation and excise duties. VAT harmonisation is seen as particularly important since the Six agreed that from 1975 the yield of up to a 1 per cent rate of VAT should be available, if required, as a source of revenue for the Community budget. While the harmonisation of tax structures involves great political difficulties, such as the treatment of food for VAT purposes, it is the harmonisation of rates which is the greater danger in economic terms. The EMU Resolution of 1971 envisaged that by the end of Stage I the Commission would have proposals ready for the alignment of VAT and excise duty rates. Fortunately little has been seen of these proposals. Harmonisation of tax rates reduces the freedom of national governments to adjust their domestic economies, although clearly some freedom is retained until all tax rates are fixed. The harmonisation of VAT rates would present particular difficulties for the UK.

Among fiscal measures, some can be introduced more easily, and take effect more quickly, than others. This can be particularly important in the context of demand management as the need for action can emerge quite quickly. Indirect taxes like VAT are relatively quick-acting and, in the UK, easy to change. Taxes on personal income cannot be so readily used as regulators because, for administrative reasons, changes cannot be introduced at short notice. Capital taxes and corporation tax can be changed more readily but the effects on the economy take longer to work through. While the harmonisation of direct tax rates would not pose the same difficulties for short-term demand management as the harmonisation of indirect tax rates, it would still be most unwelcome. Direct taxes are used for demand management purposes over somewhat longer periods as well as for the purpose of resource allocation and income distribution. The Community's desire to remove competitive distortions could lead it to propose the harmonisation of direct taxes. The 1971 EMU Resolution specifically refers to the harmonisation of taxes which have a direct influence on capital movements. Any tax harmonisation would restrict the ability of national governments to meet their varying economic and social objectives.

To some extent this limitation is inherent in the Community's vision of EMU which emphasises the abolition of fiscal frontiers and the free movement of goods, services, capital and people. This would require tax rates to be broadly similar throughout the Community. Complete equalisation of tax rates would not be necessary as the US example shows. However, we are moving towards a situation in which there is limited flexibility of fiscal policy in the medium term as well as the short term.

The expenditure side of the national budget is also an extremely important part of economic management. However, it has only limited use for demand management purposes as much of the expenditure, apart from transfer payments, can only be altered slowly and with difficulty. As with the revenue side, progress towards EMU is likely to restrict the extent to which expenditure policies can meet varying economic and social needs.

Until such time as there is complete freedom of capital movement in the Community and margins of fluctuation of exchange rates have been eliminated, the national governments will retain some freedom of manoeuvre in monetary policy. However monetary policy measures, such as changes in interest rates and quantitative measures like special deposits, ceilings on lending and variable reserve ratios, have delayed and uncertain effects on the domestic economy. For this reason monetary policy is not emphasised in the UK as a means of securing internal balance, but it is used to influence the movement of short-term capital across the exchanges.

Other instruments on the external side will be reduced in effectiveness. The exchange rate has already been discussed. Direct measures such as import controls, quotas, deposits and export subsidies, cannot be readily applied on trade with other member states and this trade is likely to form an increasing proportion of total trade. The use of foreign exchange reserves and international credit seem unlikely to be affected by the Community in the near future and the Community may increase the amount of credit available to the UK. In the longer term the locking of exchange rates will involve the pooling of external reserves.

There are certain other instruments that deserve mention. Control over the terms of hire purchase has been used in the past in the UK to influence the level of demand. However, the effectiveness of these controls has been reduced by the emergence of other channels of borrowing, and the EEC will only add to these. Fiscal incentives to investment are sometimes used, although it is doubtful if they have much effect on the volume of investment, as opposed to its location. In the EEC there will be pressure to harmonise these inventives to prevent competitive bidding for internationally mobile investment.

Finally, prices and incomes policy. This is not seen as a major instrument of demand management in the UK since it is hard to open up a significant gap for any length of time between price rises and wage settlements, except through the impact on wage costs of rising productivity. The EEC already imposes some limits on price policy, for example on steel prices, and, as links in the Community increase, wage earners may be unwilling to accept settlements much different from those of their counterparts in other member states. A development of this sort could raise substantial new economic problems for the UK. Under collective bargaining in the UK wage settlements tended to be reached at the national level. As a result the relationship between increases in wages and productivity, and so in prices, could vary from region to region. In fact prices within an industry do not show any marked discrepancies partly because of the equilibrating transfers made by the government between different regions, and partly because great similarity has developed over the years in firms' techniques and operations in the UK and in labour attitudes.

In the Community there is much less similarity. Possibly over time the same forces that made for similarity in the UK will be apparent in the Community. However, problems will arise if this development is preceded by attempts to harmonise money wage rates. Any such tendency would increase the divergence of price trends among the member states and increase the need for parity adjustments rather than reduce it. An even greater difficulty would arise if trade unions tried to secure the same settlement in real terms throughout the Community. There are clear signs that domestic wage agreements are closely related to price increases. If this were to happen within the Community, price trends would diverge even more rapidly and any attempt to offset this by parity changes would be rendered ineffective as the trade unions restored the reduction in real wages which follows a devaluation and which is necessary for the devaluation to work. This may sound alarmist, and so it may prove. At the moment all we can say is that any attempts to harmonise indirect tax rates would significantly reduce the government's ability to manage the level of demand in the short term. At the same time the government's control over the national economy will also be undermined by the increasing interdependence through trade of the economies of the Nine. If this interdependence were to extend to trade unions' wage demands in advance of convergence in the growth of productivity, the present problems of national economic management would be likely to increase.

In such a situation the Community would have to either abandon the objective of full employment or institute the necessary system of equilibrating transfers. The difficulty with transfers is that these would, in effect, be made to allow incomes in the recipient countries to be higher than productivity in these countries would justify. This might be tolerable if the productivity difference were relatively small, as within the UK, or if the gap between incomes and productivity were not too obviously the result of greed. But if the gap could be simply related to a determination to enjoy a Community level of income without earning it, there could well be severe protests from the countries making the transfers.

Community Economic Management

Increased rigidity and lack of effectiveness of economic instruments at the national level points to the need to develop instruments at the Community level, so that the effectiveness of national economic management is not weakened without some corresponding development and strengthening of Community management. At the moment the Community budget is a very small and inflexible instrument. As has already been mentioned, on present policies it seems unlikely to grow to more than 1 per cent of Community GNP by the end of this decade. Its revenue is largely derived from levies and duties on third country trade, and rates of levy and duty cannot be altered in response to conjunctural needs. On the expenditure side it is devoted solely to medium-term commitments, largely on agricultural policy. Overall its usefulness is restricted by a need to balance revenue and expenditure.

To make the budget into a significant instrument of economic management it would be necessary to increase its size substantially to introduce flexibility into both the revenue and the expenditure and to allow the Community budget to be unbalanced. It is not easy to establish a precise figure for the necessary size of the budget. In part this depends on the form and timing of EMU. If exchange rates were locked while there were still significant divergences in economic performance, it would be necessary to have a budget which could accommodate quickly and automatically massive transfers of resources. Similarly the demands will be large if EMU throws up some new disequilibrating factor like premature European-wide wage negotiations. Some indications of the size of such transfers have already been given. Even if EMU were delayed until problems of this sort seemed unlikely, it would still be sensible to have a budget that could meet these needs if they arose. In any case there would always be a need for a budget which could be used for the short-term demand management purposes associated with annual UK budgets. This alone points to a budget that could readily bring about annual changes in demand of at least £1,000 million (at 1973 prices) in each member state.

A budget of this sort would involve control over a range of tax rates and a large volume of expenditure. It would make little sense to try to throw the burden of adjustment on to a single tax or a single expenditure programme. This does not necessarily mean, however, that the Community budget would take over all national expenditure and revenue policies. It is possible to conceive of an arrangement under which the national governments retained responsibility for a range of programmes such as education and law and order. Such expenditure seems to generate strong local interest and there does not appear to be any economic need to centralise it. The necessary resources could be obtained through appropriate taxation. For example, certain taxes could be levied both nationally and at the Community level. On this basis the national authorities would retain some responsibility for income distribution and the allocation of resources to the provision of goods and services from the public sector, in so far as these budgetary functions can in practice be separated from that of demand management. There would in any case probably have to be some Community guidelines in these areas placing limits on the extent of variation in national policies.

Taken together these considerations could be seen to point to a Community budget approaching the relative size of the federal budget in the USA, say 10 per cent of Community GNP. Some might object that this would concentrate the thrust of management on too narrow a range of expenditure and revenue and involve insufficient automatic stabilisation at the Community level. There is some force in this. The revenue side of such a budget would be equivalent to slightly under half the yield of indirect taxes in the Community. On the expenditure side it would correspond to about 75 per cent of current transfers. It would also be essential for the Community to be able to run an unbalanced budget. This would involve the raising and managing of Community loans, which would be the responsibility of the Community central bank.

At the moment the Community has an embryo central bank in the form of the European Monetary Co-operation Fund. However, it is very much an embryo. At present it operates solely as a clearing house for interventions to maintain the snake and as the channel for the short-term credit facility. It has not even the advisory functions of the Committee of Central Bank Governors. The role of the EMCF may be expanded during Stage II of EMU. Commission proposals exist which would involve the EMCF in the pooling of reserves, the development of Community credit facilities and consultations on monetary policy, credit and interest rates. This would represent some development of its central banking activities, although it would still largely be a talking shop.[3]

In an EMU with locked exchange rates, pooled reserves and a single internal monetary policy and capital market there would have to be a single monetary authority. This authority could operate through regional reserve boards, as happens in the USA, but responsibility would effectively be centralised. The authority would have the normal responsibilities of a Central Bank such as the management of Community external reserves, intervention in foreign exchange markets, internal monetary policy, Community debt and exchange control.

Conclusions

The Community is committed to the formation by 1980 of an EMU characterised by locked exchange rates and a high degree of central economic management. Stage I has been a disappointment. Expectations were unreasonably high and the Stage I package was biased towards the monetary aspects of EMU. Looking to the future, political and economic realities may lead the Community to settle for some less extensive form of EMU in 1980 than that outlined in the 1971 Resolution. Even if this does happen, as we move towards EMU national economic policies and instruments will be replaced or supplemented by Community ones. We need to decide what will be needed and how those needs can be met. For example, how do we move from an inflexible EEC budget of less than 1 per cent of GNP to a flexible one of at least 10 per cent of GNP? The issues involved are basically those of sovereignty. EMU demands a transfer of power to Brussels and it will only be sensible to move towards EMU at a pace consistent with member states' readiness to make such a transfer. Fixing unrealistic goals only creates disillusion and frustration.

References

1. G.K. Shaw, "European Economic Integration and Stabilisation Policy", in C.S. Shoup (ed.), *Fiscal Harmonization in Common Markets,* Columbia University Press, New York 1967.
2. For further discussion of regional problems and policies, see Chapter 5.
3. For more detailed discussion of the potential role of the EMCF, see a Federal Trust-Vaces Study on the administrative machinery for EMU, published in the Journal of Common Market Studies, September 1974.

3 INTEGRATION OF CAPITAL MARKETS

Paul Woolley

There is an area of common ground in the issues raised by a consideration of monetary union on the one hand and capital market integration on the other. An assessment of the costs and benefits to the member countries of monetary union is concerned with the consequences of a single currency and the abandonment of controls on inter-member capital flows. It is therefore looking, *inter alia,* at the implications of a unique rate of interest, the scope for a more efficient allocation of capital and the redistributive effects of the resultant capital flows.

An appraisal of capital market integration is also concerned with these issues, but unlike a study of monetary union is specifically concerned with the various categories of capital flows, with the implications of the removal of controls on these different categories of capital flows and with the implications of the fence of capital controls, if it exists, between the union members and the rest of the world. Of concern also is the impact of integration on financial intermediation in the member countries and especially on the efficiency of the savings/investment process in these countries before and after monetary union. Capital market integration involves itself with the targets and instruments of monetary and debt management policies in the member countries before and after union. It is concerned with the distortions to the capital allocation process inherent in differing rates and structures of corporation tax, witholding tax, and depreciation provision: and with divergences in company law and capital market regulation for the Community as a whole, the member countries individually and particular sectors within them. The paper also investigates an area that has hitherto been entirely overlooked in the analysis of economic and monetary union: namely, the need for the co-ordination of debt management policies in the member countries in the event of moves towards full convertibility and the final locking of parities. Finally it considers the likely impact of the interpenetration of European capital markets on the United Kingdom, looking in particular at the effect on the flows of direct and portfolio investment funds both to and from non-EEC countries as well as on the UK system of financial intermediation.

In contrast to most other aspects of economic and monetary union, capital market integration has received scant attention in the literature. Some specific aspects of the subject have been widely studied, such as Eurocurrency and Eurobond markets; whereas others, such as capital controls in the EEC, the relative returns on capital and the relative efficiency of the diverse capital allocation processes in the member countries, have received little or no attention. The only general survey of the topic is by Magnifico, while Cooper has a useful summary of the more wide-ranging question of the development of an international capital market.[1]

Interest Rates and the Return on Capital

As a measure of the integration of the capital markets of two or more countries one may look at either relative movements of interest rates or the size of the inter-country capital flows. The limiting case of monetary union implies a unique rate of interest at each level of default risk throughout the union.[2] Until exchange rates between member countries are irrevocably fixed, however, and as long as exchange rate changes are expected then, even in the absence of exchange controls, taxation or administrative obstacles to international flows of funds, money interest rates are likely to differ. The return will be higher in those countries where devaluation relative to other countries is expected and vice versa. It is therefore unsatisfactory to use evidence on the interrelationship of money interest rates alone as a measure of capital market integration.

In so far as relative exchange rate changes exactly offset relative price level changes between countries then expected real interest rates will be equalised between countries in the absence of impediments to inter-country capital movements. But exchange rate changes rarely offset price changes precisely if only because the former usually move by discreet jumps. Also since expected relative rates of price change (or alternatively expected currency realignments) may prove incorrect then *ex post* real interest rates will not have been equalised. All that can be said is that *observed* real interest rates can, in general, be expected to move closer into line as obstacles to capital flows are progressively removed. From the evidence for the principal EEC countries over the last twelve years in Table 1, no clear trend towards convergence of real interest rates is apparent.[3]

Within a single economy capital, whether in the form of direct or portfolio investment funds, is free to move from industry to industry and from firm to firm. If the capital market is efficient investment funds will be allocated to industries and projects in such a way that the expected future returns on new investment throughout the economy will be equalised at the margin at every level of risk. Of course the capital

TABLE 1

	GERMANY			FRANCE			ITALY			NETHERLANDS			BELGIUM			U.K.		
	r	i	(r-i)	r	i	(r-i)	r	i	(r-i)	r	i	(r-i)	r	i	(r-i)	r	i	(r-i)
1960	6.4	1.0	5.4	5.1	3.8	1.3	5.2	2.0	3.2	4.2	1.0	3.2	5.5	1.0	4.5	5.4	1.0	4.4
1961	5.9	2.9	3.0	5.1	3.6	1.5	5.2	1.9	3.3	3.9	1.9	2.0	5.9	1.0	4.9	6.2	2.9	3.3
1962	5.9	3.2	2.7	5.0	4.4	0.6	5.3	4.6	0.7	4.2	2.1	2.1	5.2	1.0	4.2	6.0	4.3	1.7
1963	6.0	3.1	2.9	5.0	5.3	-0.3	5.4	7.5	-2.1	4.2	4.2	0.0	5.0	3.1	1.9	5.6	2.0	3.6
1964	6.2	2.0	4.2	5.1	3.0	2.1	6.3	6.0	0.3	4.9	6.0	-1.1	5.6	3.0	2.6	6.0	3.0	3.0
1965	7.0	3.7	3.3	5.3	2.9	2.4	5.7	4.4	1.3	5.2	3.5	1.7	5.6	5.2	0.4	6.4	5.0	1.4
1966	8.1	3.4	4.7	5.4	2.7	2.7	6.5	2.4	4.1	6.2	7.0	-0.8	6.6	4.2	2.4	6.9	3.9	3.0
1967	7.0	1.7	5.3	5.7	2.8	2.9	6.6	3.6	3.0	6.0	3.4	2.6	6.7	2.9	3.8	6.8	2.5	4.3
1968	6.5	1.5	5.0	5.9	4.5	1.4	6.7	3.4	3.3	6.2	3.6	2.6	6.5	2.8	3.7	7.5	4.7	2.8
1969	6.8	2.7	4.1	7.6	6.2	1.4	6.8	6.4	0.4	7.0	7.4	-0.4	7.2	3.7	3.5	9.0	5.4	3.6
1970	8.3	3.9	4.4	8.1	5.5	2.6	9.0	4.9	4.1	7.8	3.6	4.2	7.8	3.9	3.9	9.2	6.4	2.8
1971	8.0	5.1	2.9	7.7	5.6	2.1	8.3	4.8	3.5	7.0	7.5	-0.5	7.3	4.4	2.9	8.9	9.5	-0.6
1972	7.9	5.8	2.1	7.3	5.8	1.5	7.5	5.7	1.8	6.7	7.8	-1.1	7.0	5.4	1.6	8.9	7.1	1.8

r = money rates of return p.a.
i = rate of price inflation p.a.
(r-i) gives 'real' rate of return p.a.

Sources: International Financial Statistics: Government Bond Yield
Consumer Price Index

market may not be efficient, capital may move only sluggishly, monopolistic elements may distort the allocation process and information about opportunities may not be widely disseminated. If two or more countries form a monetary union the argument is that there are potential gains stemming from a more efficient allocation of capital between the member countries. Prior to monetary union the existence of capital controls, differences in corporate tax structure and rates, withholding taxes, and information deficiencies prevented the equalisation of expected marginal returns on capital at each level of risk. The greater the initial divergence in these marginal returns the greater the potential benefit deriving from economic and monetary union. Note, however, that since long-term investment in real assets is not susceptible to exchange rate risk, monetary union does not offer a gain in this context.

Any actual assessment of the potential gain from the reallocation of capital within the EEC encounters serious problems. First, it is the *expected* returns that are equated and it is notoriously difficult to observe expectations. Secondly, it is returns at the *margin* that are relevant and while some estimates of average returns might be possible the former are less amenable to estimation. Thirdly, a measure of the assumed risk class is required and this is not straightforward. Finally, there is a dearth of data on returns on capital in the EEC. Using data on the average return over the years 1969-71 on capital employed in publicly quoted industrial and commercial firms (but excluding financial concerns) in the member countries, the ordering in descending magnitudes is as in column (1). Columns (2) and (3) give the rankings using the same ratios for similar periods for UK and US firms operating in these countries.

	(1) EEC firms	(2) UK firms	(3) US firms
Germany	1	1	1
France	2	3	6
UK	3	-	3
Belgium	4	4	2
Netherlands	5	2	4
Italy	6	5	5

Since flows of direct investment funds within the EEC have been relatively free from controls for a number of years, one is inclined to the view that the potential gains from reallocation of capital following monetary union are not great.

Capital Flows and Controls[4]

Capital flows may be categorised according to the end-use of the investment (direct, portfolio, property), the type of lender (public, personal, corporate) or the duration of the investment (short-term, long-term). As an indicator of the degree of interpenetration of the capital markets of the two countries it is gross rather than net flows that are significant. While quantitative data can be used to investigate whether the capital markets of different countries are more or less integrated over time with respect to a given category of capital flow there is no level of flow that represents full integration and it is arbitrary to give equal weight to fund flows in different categories.

Controls on flows of capital into or out of a country may be imposed to satisfy a number of objectives. They may be imposed to influence the aggregate inflow or outflow of private capital, whether domestic or foreign-owned, so as to correct a balance-of-payments deficit or surplus. Or, as an extension of this, controls may be imposed in order to maintain an exchange rate at a level other than that which would prevail under free market conditions. They may be imposed on specific categories of flows in an attempt to influence the composition of the balance of payments, or to influence capital flows to or from specific countries. For these two reasons controls may be imposed on both inflows *and* outflows at any one time by any one country. Controls may be applied to protect an inefficient capital market or to further a policy of planned rather than market allocation of capital. Whatever the rationale, the effectiveness of an independent monetary policy is circumscribed in the absence of exchange controls.

The controls themselves may be divided broadly into two groups:[5] the market-oriented and the legally or administratively based. Into the first category falls the two-tier exchange rate in which the financial rate is at a premium or a discount to the official rate depending on the balance of supply and demand for currency for capital transactions between the country in question and the rest of the world. This rate may float cleanly or be subject to intervention by the authorities. A version of this is the two-tier rate in which the capital rate depends on the supply and demand for foreign currency for capital transactions by residents alone or domestic currency by foreigners alone. Restrictions on interest payments on non-resident bank deposits is another market-oriented device in so far as it does not prevent the flows taking place but only reduces their attraction. The more administrative types of controls include: restrictions on foreign investment in domestic securities or domestic investment in foreign securities; restrictions on bank deposits held by non-residents; ceilings or minimum reserve requirements for non-resident bank deposits; restrictions on residents' deposits in foreign countries.

In a number of ways they resemble tariffs on goods, but with some significant differences. The export of capital may encounter a control on the outflow as well as a control on the inflow into the host country although the second control may compound or offset the first. While a tariff involves a single known cost, the exporter or importer of capital is concerned not only with the capital controls on the initial flow but the control or probability of a control being in force when the income, interest payments or capital itself are expected to be repatriated. Like tariffs, however, exchange controls imposed by one country impinge on the balance of payments, growth rate, etc. of other countries. For this reason controls may be imposed as a retaliatory measure.

If exchange controls are lifted by two or more countries with respect to each other but retained independently with respect to third countries, a counterpart to a free trade area in goods has been formed for capital. There will similarly be gains and losses in the reallocation of capital corresponding to trade creation and trade diversion. The different controls with respect to their countries can cause capital to flow into the free capital area through the country with the lowest inflow controls and to flow out of the area through the country with the lowest controls on outflows. Policing of capital movements with regard to origin and destination is more difficult than for goods. If there is a common external fence of capital controls then this problem is avoided. In fact if a number of countries form a monetary union it would be virtually impossible to enforce anything other than a common external fence.

Attention has already been drawn to the potential benefits to a single country from the operation of capital controls. There may even be benefits to two or more countries if one or more of them imposes controls on the flows of funds between them. This argument derives from the theory of the 'second best' and rests on the hypothesis that because of an existing market imperfection, the allocation process is improved by the retention of capital controls. There is also the possibility that for two or more countries moving towards monetary union, capital controls contribute usefully to the regional distribution of income.

The Treaty of Rome committed member countries progressively to abolish restrictions on intra-EEC capital movements to the extent necessary to ensure 'proper functioning of the Common Market'.[6] The obligations which the member states have agreed to accept regarding capital flows were spelled out in two Community Directives in 1960 and 1962. Briefly, capital flows were categorised under four headings:

List A.   Direct investment, purchase of property, commercial credit and personal remittance.

List B. Portfolio investment.

List C. Issues of securities on other national capital markets by Community residents.

List D. Short-term money and bill market investment flows, personal loans.

Member governments are required to guarantee provision of foreign exchange for transactions included in List A, and with certain exemptions, for those in List B as well. It is interesting to note that, for both these categories, the possibility of maintaining some forms of exchange control is not excluded. Governments are required to ensure that, where a two-tier exchange rate exists, the financial rate should not differ 'substantially' from the official rate. Hence the option is left open for dual markets of the type operated for many years by Belgium and more recently adopted by France, Italy and also for the existence of the investment currency market in the United Kingdom. For List C, the Directive froze exchange control regulations as they then obtained. Thus while the option was there for countries to liberalise transactions in these areas, there was a corresponding right to withdraw any concessions made since that time if balance-of-payments considerations should dictate. For List D, controls were left to the discretion of member governments.

Following these directives, there was a widespread lifting of controls in the early and mid-1960s. A feature of these steps was that in almost all cases measures towards liberalisation were applied equally to non-members. This should be borne in mind when assessing the extent of integration as measured by capital flows. In any investigation of the capital flows within the EEC and the effect of reduced barriers on movements of capital, it is necessary to study not how they increased over time but to try and answer the more difficult question of how they compare at any point in time with the size they might have been without the formation of the EEC. R.G. Hawkins,[7] using aggregate data for private long-term capital flows between 1960 and 1967, found conflicting evidence. As a proportion of capital inflows intra-EEC movements tended to increase while as a proportion of capital outflows they tended to decline. Data was not available with which to appraise the degree of change in the interdependence of EEC money markets.

The progress made in removing barriers to free capital movement came to a sudden end with the international monetary crisis in 1968 to 1969. Controls imposed then have remained, although their precise form and severity have varied. Table 2 indicates the principal controls that existed for each of the main EEC member countries at the end of 1973. It is clear that members are divided between those that in general encourage inflows and/or discourage outflows (United Kingdom, Italy and France); while Germany, the Netherlands and Belgium currently discourage inflows and/or encourage outflows. Of course the position of each country could easily shift or even be reversed following a major parity change. Though controls only impede movement in one direction the effect is to restrict more than half the potential flows because the direction of the desired net flow is against the controls. The other feature of the present pattern of controls is that it is directed in the main against portfolio investment and short-term capital flows, leaving direct investment flows more or less unaffected. This accords with the philosophy of seeking to contain speculative and disruptive capital flows and the general preference for direct investment as opposed to portfolio investment flows by both exporting and host countries. Nevertheless, the desire of each country to assert its claim to be the financial centre of Europe encourages each to adopt as liberal an attitude as possible to portfolio investment and flows of short-term funds.

In the Report of the EEC Commission to the Council in April 1973 it was stated that: 'For freedom of movement for capital to be gradually established the Community as a whole must adopt the same type of strategy towards the outside world. The member states should have equal protection as regards movements of capital to and from the outside world. This will make it possible to establish progressively different sets of rules for capital movements within the community and for those involving non-member countries, in particular reducing to a minimum administrative controls on the former and by relying in their case on systems of dissuasion.' A common fence of controls would avoid the problems associated with an uneven fence and although no mention has been made of the nature of the common control arrangement, the claims of a dual rate system or a version of it and such a system can be shown to be, on balance, more effective, more equitable, efficient and flexible than alternative systems of control.[8] There is of course the problem of equity in so far as controls on capital flows are traditionally observed conscientiously in some member countries but casually in others.

If the Commission also has in mind the dual rate for intra-EEC capital controls, as the alternative to administrative controls, there would be a prospect of three exchange rates for each member country. Policing problems would certainly arise, although the UK effectively survived such a regime when there were two investment currency premiums for a number of years. It is to be presumed that intra-EEC capital controls are being retained as a supporting instrument of regional policy and/or as a corrective device for any imperfection that makes full mobility of capital at a single exchange rate non-optimal. In this event, the imposition of the controls should be at the discretion of the central EEC authority rather than subject to the manipulation of the member countries. Also the controls need to be evaluated against

TABLE 2

Capital controls in force in the principal member
countries of EEC at the end of 1973

Measures	Country / Currently Operating To Influence	GERMANY		FRANCE		ITALY		N'LANDS		BELGIUM		U.K.	
Type	Description	in-flows	out-flows	in-flows	out-flows	in-flows	out-flows	in-flows	out-flows	in-flows	out-flows	in-flows	out-flows
1. Market Oriented	Floating 'financial' or 'capital' rate				x		x				x		
	Investment currency markets of restricted size							x					x
	Restriction of interest payments on non-resident bank deposits	x						x		x			
2. Legal or Administrative	Restrictions on foreign investments in domestic securities	x											
	Restrictions on bank deposits held by non-residents							x		x			
	Ceilings or minimum reserve requirements for non-resident bank deposits	x									x		
	Restrictions on residents' deposits in foreign countries				†						†		
3. Others	Favourable attitude toward foreign borrowing by domestic public bodies												
	Favourable attitude to foreign borrowing on domestic capital market								†				

x – Denotes discouragement
† – Denotes encouragement

alternative, and possibly more selective, instruments as regards effectiveness, efficiency, and equity. On the other hand they may simply be regarded as a feature of the transitional period and an accompaniment to the exchange controls that will also have to be applied as the Europa is introduced.

Future policy towards intra-EEC controls must be considered in conjunction with the whole question of exchange rate policy and steps towards economic union. The renunciation of the right to control capital flows is part of the fundamental issue of the emergence of an EEC welfare function. An EEC welfare function may be thought of not as replacing the national welfare functions but rather as augmenting them at a higher level in the same way that a national welfare function presently tops a pyramid of such functions that include region, locality, firm and family.

Capital Markets: Characteristics and Policies

In this section we outline the characteristics of the capital markets in the various member countries and the policies adopted towards them by the respective monetary authorities. We then consider the relative efficiency with which the capital allocation systems operate in the different countries. This comparative approach forms the basis of the analysis in the following section of the processes of financial intermediation and capital allocation in an integrated European capital market.

Table 3 below gives some idea of the relative sizes of the capital markets in the member countries.

TABLE 3

Gross Savings in Eight EEC Countries
and the United States

Country	Gross Savings in 1971 (US $ (billions) valued at exchange rate of July, 1973)	Gross Savings as percentage of GNP (average 1967-71)
Belgium	10.2	24.7
Denmark	4.3	19.5
France	60.1	28.0
Germany	87.7	27.5
Ireland	0.9	18.5
Italy	24.0	23.2
Netherlands	13.0	27.5
United Kingdom	28.9	18.5
EEC	Total 229.1	
c.f United States	259.9	24.7

Sources: OECD Financial Statistics; IMF International Financial Statistics

The table shows gross savings in each of the member countries in 1971 and gross savings as a percentage of gross national product averaged over the years 1967-71. Germany and France are together shown to account for almost two-thirds of the entire volume of savings in the EEC. The figure for the United Kingdom seems surprisingly small but it must be remembered that the size of the capital market in a country may be greater than is suggested by the figure for gross domestic savings because of international financial intermediation undertaken there. The figures also reveal that the combined gross savings of EEC member countries is only slightly smaller than that for the United States.

The system of capital allocation differs strikingly among the major EEC economies.[9] In France the savings-investment process is dominated by government-controlled financial institutions which allocate capital according to the priorities perceived by the authorities and in line with the dictates of the national plan. The role of private insurance companies, pension funds, unit and investment trusts in France is limited, and they are in any case obliged to channel a large proportion of their funds through state agencies. State institutions also dominate the long-term bond market and private industry relies heavily on these institutions as a source of finance. The situation is similar in Italy where autonomous government agencies and special credit institutions controlled by publicly-owned banks play the dominant role in channelling capital to industrial investment.

The German capital market is dominated by multi-role private sector commercial banks. In addition to the provision of loans to the corporate sector these banks have large equity holdings and use their shareholdings to exercise control over corporate management. They also constitute the membership of the stock exchange and own and manage the mutual funds. While the banks are not subject to direct government intervention they wield their considerable oligopolistic power so as not to come into direct conflict with the objectives of the authorities.

In contrast to both the French and German systems the savings-investment processes in the United Kingdom and the Netherlands are characterised by a more market-oriented approach with a large number of private sector financial intermediaries competing for turnover and profit and little or no intervention by financial institutions in the management of industrial concerns. Of course the authorities can still influence the capital allocation process by means of fiscal incentives and directives to the intermediaries concerning their lending policies. The private sector in the United Kingdom has in the past relied on public issues of bonds and equities as a source of finance to a much greater extent than the private sectors of other member countries. This is apparent from the relative size of outstanding issues of corporate equities in the principal EEC countries as set out in Table 4. The comparable figures for bonds are unfortunately not available.

TABLE 4

Market capitalisation of quoted equities at the end of 1971

	£1000 millions
Belgium	2.68
France	9.57
Germany	13.30
Italy	4.00
Netherlands	5.31
United Kingdom	41.00

Despite the differing approaches to capital allocation in the member countries, the current demands of the corporate sector upon the new issue market are no greater relatively in the United Kingdom than elsewhere (see Table 5 below). In fact new public issues of corporate bonds and equities as a proportion of GNP in the UK have for some years now been smaller than in any other EEC member country, apart from the Netherlands.

TABLE 5

Public issues of corporate securities (bonds and equities) as a percentage of GNP

Year	1967	1968	1969	1970	1971
Belgium	3.3	4.7	3.4	5.5	5.9
France	2.4	2.4	2.5	2.8	3.1
Germany	3.1	3.8	3.0	2.9	3.2
Italy	5.3	N/A	6.1	5.6	N/A
Netherlands	0.5	0.7	0.6	1.0	N/A
United Kingdom	0.7	1.2	1.1	0.4	0.6

Wide differences exist in the method of capital market regulation in the member countries. The purpose of this regulation is broadly to implement monetary, fiscal and debt management policies, but also to protect investors, to influence the capital allocation process, to ensure 'orderly' financial markets and to influence the degree of competition among financial intermediaries. In the United Kingdom, for example, there is an absence of the codified system of regulation of banks that is a feature of most other EEC countries. Instead the authorities in the

United Kingdom rely on a system of conventions, moral suasion and the prudence of investors and the financial institutions themselves.

Such an arrangement may be contrasted with the stringent banking codes in Germany and France which prescribe the scope of commercial banking activities and the manner in which they are to be performed. Similarly the investment policies of insurance companies, mutual funds and pension funds are more tightly controlled on the Continent than in the United Kingdom. The contrast is also apparent in the extent to which the United Kingdom capital market relies on self-policing (by the Stock Exchange Council, Take-Over Panel, etc.) rather than regulation by government bodies.

The efficiency of a capital market is most commonly defined in terms of the 'optimal' allocation of investment funds in the sense that scarce resources are allocated to those uses that are expected to yield the highest return. One of the tests for the efficiency of the stock market according to this definition is whether or not security prices follow a random walk. But we have observed that stock markets in Europe play a relatively small role in the overall savings-investment process in each country. No test has yet been devised to investigate the efficient allocation of capital in an entire economy. One might hypothesise that, in the same way as the existence of competing participants in the stock market ensures the efficiency of security prices, so the existence of a large number of competing financial intermediaries in an economy will ensure the optimal allocation of resources in the entire market for capital in a country. It is also suggested that the growth rate of the economy is an indicator of the efficiency of the allocative process, although there is the familiar problem of holding other factors constant.

On the criterion of competing financial intermediaries the United Kingdom certainly scores well in contrast to the oligopolistic banking structure in Germany and the government-controlled capital markets in France and Italy, yet it scores badly on the growth-rate comparison. In explanation it is argued that a market-oriented financial system is concerned with private, rather than social, costs and benefits; encourages short time-horizons and inevitably lays excessive emphasis on share-price maximisation, asset stripping and similar financial operations at the expense of the real investment projects that underlie them. It is also the case that there are imperfections in the United Kingdom capital market that the new 'Competition and Credit Policy' of 1971 only went some way to correcting. The integration of the financial and industrial sectors in Germany may be an important factor in ensuring an efficient allocation of capital while the merit of the French system may lie in the account taken of social rather than purely private benefits.

The efficiency of capital markets may also be defined in terms of the resource cost of the financial intermediation process, the responsiveness of monetary target variables to government policy measures and the extent to which lenders and borrowers are provided with financial assets and liabilities that are most preferred with regard to risk, return, liquidity and maturity. The relative merits of the different systems on the first criterion is an empirical question and cannot be established *a priori.* On the second, a government-controlled system is probably more efficient than its market-oriented counterpart in which intermediaries consistently seek to minimise the impact of monetary restrictions that conflict with the firms' profit objectives. With regard to the third criterion, stringent regulation of financial intermediaries can be expected to inhibit innovation in the creation of financial instruments and the more liberal approach to the control of capital markets may be preferable. A rather different aspect of efficiency is the orderliness of markets and effectively protecting investors. The recurrent crises in the secondary banking and insurance sectors in the United Kingdom suggest that the liberal approach also has its drawbacks.

It would not be possible to discuss capital markets in Europe without mentioning the Eurocurrency and Eurobond markets that have developed strongly since the early 1960s. These markets have been an important element in linking the capital markets of the member countries. Their characteristics have been extensively analysed elsewhere[10] and the features that have attracted particular attention are the Eurocurrency multiplier, the extent to which these markets have narrowed the yield differentials between countries, the absence of official regulation, the problems that have beset the secondary market in Eurobonds and the role played in their development by the US balance-of-payments deficit.

The Integrated Capital Market

The necessary conditions for a fully integrated EEC capital market are irrevocably locked exchange rates, the absence of exchange controls, the absence of other deterrents to intra-EEC capital flows, whether administrative, fiscal or legal (except in so far as such controls or deterrents are an explicit arm of regional, industrial or social policy), the freedom of establishment for financial intermediaries, and the freedom of provision of financial services within the Union by firms based in another member country.

There would probably be more or less general agreement about the characteristics of the ideal, fully-integrated EEC capital market. These would include:

(1)   an efficient market in the sense that the savings-investment

process produced a socially optimal allocation of capital
for the community as a whole;

(2)   the absence of monopoly profits for financial intermediaries;

(3)   the responsiveness of monetary variables to policy regulation
by the central authorities in the EEC;

(4)   'low' resource cost of financial intermediation.

There would, however, be disagreement among economists and more
particularly among representatives of the member countries about how
this state of affairs should be achieved. Following the distributional
implications of the alternative strategies, disagreement would derive in
part from the self-interest of the countries concerned and of the pressure
groups within them. Disagreement would also stem from differing
theoretical judgements and differing political standpoints. Each country
would be likely to press for the adoption of its own system of capital
allocation and of capital market regulation as the model for the EEC as
a whole.

Before considering these issues further there are several analytical
points that can be made about the consequences of satisfying the
necessary conditions for full capital market integration. Firstly
integration enhances utility by providing individuals and companies
(and therefore individuals indirectly) with potentially more preferred
types of financial assets and liabilities. Companies are given access to a
wider range of financial liabilities, and larger issues can be made on a
trans-EEC capital market than on the domestic market alone. Financial
assets become more liquid because a larger market exists for each type.
Against these gains must be set one source of lower utility. International
investment, whether direct or portfolio, typically offers scope for risk
reduction because of the low level of convertibility between investment
returns in different countries. Integration in the goods and factors
markets of the Community will give rise to more positive covariance
between investment returns in the member countries. There will thus
be a reduced scope for risk reduction from investing funds in another
member country and therefore lower utility from all portfolios, whether
belonging to EEC or non-EEC investors, that include holdings in more
than one EEC country. Risk reduction can be secured again by
switching some funds to securities or projects outside the Community
and we thus have the prediction that capital market integration will, on
one score at least, tend to promote an outflow of capital.

The second piece of analysis concerns cross-frontier competition in
financial intermediation. Before the integration of the capital markets
of countries forming an economic and monetary union, financial
intermediaries in one country will not have unrestricted access to the
capital markets of other member countries. It may be the case that
financial intermediaries in one or several of the member countries

command monopoly power that gives rise to excessive profits, an absence of innovation, or inefficiency in the sense of a high opportunity cost of the resources used in the savings-investment process. Once the obstacles to cross-frontier interpenetration by financial intermediaries are lifted, then greater competition will be likely to eliminate these manifestations of monopoly power. The further question of whether more competition will improve the efficiency of the capital allocation process itself depends on the view taken about the relative merits of different systems. The EEC Commission is working towards the removal of obstacles to interpenetration by banks and insurance companies and will soon be moving on to look at other financial intermediaries. Of course there is the possibility of oligopolistic collusion among the banks, for example, in the various countries in the form of agreements not to compete in each other's territory or alternatively of cross-frontier mergers that will recreate monopoly power. In fact, loose multinational consortia of banks have already been set up, though collusion is unlikely to survive an active anti-monopoly policy at EEC level.

A rather special type of financial intermediary is the stock exchange. The stock exchange in a country usually commands a monopoly in so far as it is necessary to go through a member of a unified body in order to buy or sell bonds or securities. The monopoly arises from the difficulty of providing an alternative market in which the probability of being able to find a buyer or a seller for a security is as high as in the existing market. The monopoly is usually compounded by collusion among brokers over minimum commission charges. If exchange control and other obstacles to the free flow of portfolio investment funds (and the trans-frontier issue of new bonds and securities) are lifted, then it seems that the various national stock exchanges will each be competing through efficiency and lower commission charges for becoming the principal market for the shares of the larger companies which will be increasingly held on a Europe-wide scale. The end result will probably be a 'Trans-EEC Stock Exchange' with unified rules for quotation and operation, but it would be unfortunate if there was not at the same time competitive pricing of brokers' services within it.[11]

Another potential efficiency gain stems from the scope that integration of capital markets provides for cross-frontier take-overs in the commercial and industrial field. At present such take-overs are impeded by legal, administrative and fiscal obstacles, although these obstacles are gradually being broken down by appropriate community directives. With their removal, inefficient firms in one country will become exposed to take-overs by more efficient firms in another member country. This suggests opportunities for improving the productivity of *existing* capital in addition to the efficiency gains from the reallocation of *new* capital. On the other hand, one might legitimately question why inefficient firms have not already been acquired by others in their own country (unless all firms in a country are inefficient) or how this gain differs from the competitive stimulus stemming from the dismantling of tariff barriers. Empirical studies have questioned the effectiveness of take-overs in enhancing efficiency[12] and there are cogent arguments against financial manipulation, especially by conglomerates, which are likely to be used as a defence against some UK take-overs of continental firms. Finally, there is the danger of take-over merely to achieve monopoly, and greater productivity does not necessarily represent an increase in welfare.

Integration may be accomplished by two routes, the choice depending on the degree of segmentation of the domestic markets. In the first case domestic financial markets may be highly integrated and efficient and without obvious distortion, regulation or monopoly. In this situation the freeing of all barriers to intra-union flows of funds in only one submarket (say the money market) will accomplish a high degree of integration in *all* the financial markets. Observe that the barriers to be removed include not only the obvious exchange controls but also the discriminatory portfolio regulations, fiscal deterrents, legal obstacles and so forth. On the other hand domestic markets may be compartmentalised, with little communication between submarkets, in which case the above approach will not satisfactorily integrate the capital markets as a whole. Thus either the domestic markets can be rationalised and integration can then take place via one or two submarkets, *or* intra-union barriers can be lifted with respect to each financial submarket while leaving the degree of domestic market segmentation unchanged. The Segré Report recognised the close approximation of the countries then constituting the EEC to the second situation and recommended that a broad range of members' submarkets be integrated in parallel. Certainly submarkets within the national capital markets, except those of the United Kingdom and the Netherlands, tend to be compartmentalised, resulting in a sluggish transmission of credit pressures from one segment to another and a slow and constrained accommodation between excess supply and demand for funds in submarkets. At present we have seen that the member countries are not prepared to remove capital controls on all categories of flows and that controls are most stringent on those that are potentially most disruptive, namely the short-term flows. (The fact that long-term and direct investment fund flows are imperfect substitutes for short-term flows explains why there is not an equally restrictive approach to all categories of fund flows and why there is compartmentalisation of domestic capital markets in the first place.) The approach that is in general being adopted is to free intra-EEC flows until there is a greater degree of political and economic integration. This seems the appropriate strategy for attaining the ultimate target of complete integration.

Consider the situation in which full capital mobility is introduced between two countries in one of which capital is allocated largely according to government direction while the other has a market-based system of capital allocation. After Union either central planning in the first country tends to be defeated by market forces, or if control over the allocation process is successfully retained by this country then there has not effectively been a full integration of the two capital markets. Monetary union in fact requires a surrender of the control of monetary policy to the Union central bank and this must be accompanied by a surrender to the centre of the principal instruments of government control over the capital allocation process. This applies not only to the explicit directives that are part of the French and Italian systems but also to the fiscal incentives and subsidised rates of interest that are used by all governments to influence the allocation of capital. Some autonomy for the member countries in these matters is possible, and indeed desirable, but excessive decentralisation of power here would run counter to the principles of monetary union and conflict with the objective of freely competitive markets. The fully integrated European capital market that eventually emerges may well be closer to the market-oriented than the centrally planned system because the former would be more in accordance with the philosophies of both the Treaty of Rome and the majority of member countries and it would be difficult ever to obtain agreement among member governments about the optimal allocation of capital under a planned system.

Close to this issue is the question of the harmonisation of the instruments of monetary policy in general prior to the transfer of most, if not all, to the EEC central bank with the advent of monetary union. This is already called for in some measure by the move on the part of the Community to introduce freedom of establishment for financial intermediaries and freedom for the provision of their services within the Community. The latter objective in particular requires that there is a harmonisation of the system of control of intermediaries throughout the EEC, with the banking sector one of the most significant in this respect. In the unification of banking regulations the outcome is likely to be a compromise between the liberalism of the UK and the rigid codes that exist on the Continent.

Monetary union and capital market integration redistribute income and wealth. The difficulty of achieving both in fact stems largely from their redistributional effects between member countries. For example, capital mobility lowers the expected return to investment in relatively high-yield countries and conversely. It also reduces the return to labour in those countries from which there is an outflow of capital (or creates unemployment if wages are rigid downwards) and vice versa. The impact on the tax yield of the individual countries is complex and cannot be specified *a priori*. As with all other aspects of economic and monetary union it is impossible to consider capital market integration in isolation. Regional policy is concerned with correcting regional disparities in income, employment and welfare. One way of doing this is to give tax incentives or provide loans at subsidies rates of interest to firms investing in specific areas. In so far as the allocation of capital is changed from what it would otherwise have been, then this is a common concern of capital market policy. Similarly industrial policy is concerned with the conditions of efficiency, competiton and monopoly in industry and with fostering the development of EEC-wide co-operation in certain capital-intensive activities. Capital market policy is relevant here since the efficiency of capital markets and their ability to provide large-scale finance are important prerequisites for these objectives. Again, since capital flows influence the returns to labour and the availability and conditions of work, capital market policy impinges on territory that is of central concern to social policy.

Debt Management[13]

A fundamental aspect of capital market policy in any country is the manner in which the authorities manage the public debt. It can be shown that economic and monetary integration in the EEC will have far-reaching implications for the future of public debt management in the member countries. Yet, surprisingly, there appears to have been no consideration of them at either the academic or policy-making level. One possible explanation of this oversight is that debt management falls uneasily between the now well-worked fields of monetary unification and fiscal harmonisation. At present each country manipulates the size and maturity structure of its national debt by its own particular methods, and to its own desired ends, quite independently of its fellow EEC members. However, as progress is made towards monetary union, so there will have to be a parallel advance in the co-ordination of debt management policies. The achievement of the goal of a common currency will require the transfer from the separate national authorities to the Community of the power of approval for all public debt issues and redemptions, as well as for variations in the maturity structure of each country's outstanding debt. The monetary authorities in the Community will then begin to operate their own debt policy for stabilisation and, presumably, also for budgetary purposes.

National debt can be defined in several ways. A broad definition would include all claims against the government held by the private sector, in which case it would encompass not only the sum of all outstanding bonds and bills of all maturities but also currency and the deposit obligations of the central bank. A narrower definition would exclude the monetary base and confine itself to government bonds, from the short-term to the undated. The size of the debt, as broadly defined, is the result of past and current fiscal policies, since a budget deficit will increase the government's obligations to the private sector while surpluses will reduce them. If we use this broad definition, the composition of the debt is an area of common ground for both monetary and debt management policies since both will be concerned with the size of the monetary base. If we adopt the second and narrower definition of debt and accept that monetary policy determines the monetary base, and therefore the general level of interest rates, then the province of debt management is restricted to the composition and not the size of the bond issue. Although we are concerned with the bond issue here rather than the money supply, we will be looking not only at the maturity composition but also at the size of debt as narrowly defined.

There are marked differences between the EEC countries both in the absolute size of central government debt and in its size relative to other magnitudes, such as gross national product. However, problems of comparability arise in attempting to provide a common delineation of central government debt, particularly in respect of bond issues of nationalised industries and government-controlled credit institutions. The treatment of interdepartmental holdings of government stock and the valuation of unquoted issues is also troublesome. With these caveats we give in Table 6 both the market capitalisation in sterling terms of the central government debt of each of the member countries and its value as a proportion of the gross national product.

TABLE 6

Size of central government debt in various EEC countries
in 1970

	Absolute size (£ million)	Size relative to GNP in 1970
United Kingdom	33,079	65%
Belgium	5,163	43%
France	7,413	11%
Germany	9,475	7%
Italy	6,410	41%
Netherlands	3,792	29%

(Sources: EEC General Statistics: Annual Abstract)

These figures show that the United Kingdom has by far the largest central government debt both in absolute terms and as a proportion of GNP, and reflect the Exchequer's past preference for bond finance as opposed to taxation as a source of revenue. Important contributors to the debt have been war financing and nationalisation.

As a measure of current demands made by each government on its capital market, Table 7 shows the net domestic borrowing as a percentage of government revenue over the period 1966-71.

TABLE 7

Net domestic borrowing as a proportion of government revenue in various EEC countries, 1966-71

	Per cent
United Kingdom	5.4
Belgium	12.1
France	3.8
Germany	4.5
Italy	24.4
Netherlands	8.8

(Source: International Financial Statistics)

The United Kingdom, Germany and France are more or less equally reliant on bond finance relative to other forms of government revenue, but Italy and Belgium make proportionately much larger demands on the capital market. The reason for Italy's heavy reliance on debt finance may well have something to do with the problems of raising taxes at both the personal and the corporate level.

Turning to the maturity composition of the debt, an important difference between the composition of the central government debt in the United Kingdom and that in all other member countries, except possibly the Netherlands, is the relatively large share of bonds which have more than twenty years to run or are irredeemable. Because of the absence of fully comparable data, Table 8 unfortunately fails to show this difference as clearly as one would like.

TABLE 8

Maturity structure of central government debt in EEC countries, 1972

Maturity (years)	0-5 %	5-10 %	10-20 %	Over 20 and undated %
United Kingdom	29	14	39	18
Belgium	24		76	
France	80		20	
Germany	5		95	
Italy	50		50	
Netherlands	7	23	69	1

(*Sources:* EEC General Statistics; Netherlands Treasury; UK Stock Exchange Fact Book)

The absence of long-dated bonds in a country undoubtedly reflects deficiencies on the demand rather than on the supply side. This hypothesis is consistent with the fact that in the private sectors of both the United Kingdom and the Netherlands, financial intermediaries, such as pension funds and life assurance companies, with long-term commitments and therefore with a preference for investments of matching maturity, are in a more advanced stage of development than elsewhere.

There is a further difference in the characteristics of the bonds issued in the various countries. In Italy and the Netherlands a large proportion are redeemable by random drawings rather than at some predetermined date. The redemption yield on such bonds is thus not known with complete certainty.

The authorities in the United Kingdom altered their policy towards the gilt-edged market at the time of the introduction of competition and credit control in May 1971. This signalled a change of emphasis in the priorities accorded to the various objectives and also a change in the instruments used to achieve them. According to the Bank of England[14] the principal concern of debt management is 'to encourage the widest possible variety of investors, other than banks, to increase their holdings and to hold longer rather than shorter-dated stock.' This is also seen as an aspect of credit policy since it ensures that the government's financing needs can be met with less recourse to the banks, and consequently a smaller addition to the banks' liquid assets and less scope for them to increase their lending. Another aim of debt management is to assist economic policy by promoting and sustaining the most appropriate pattern of interest rates. Two further objectives are the determination of the proportionate share of net bond issues made by the central government, the local authorities and corporate borrowers in each maturity category and the minimisation of interest cost of debt service to the Exchequer.

Now it is evident that some of these targets are mutually conflicting. Thus the authorities are obliged to choose between them according to the circumstances at the time. For example, cost minimisation will almost certainly conflict with the achievement of the desired pattern of interest rates: monetising the debt would eliminate the interest cost but only at the expense of hyperinflation.

It is thought that marketability of gilt-edged stocks and the minimum of short-term fluctuations are important for the achievement of maximum bond sales. Before 1971 there was large-scale intervention by the authorities in the market for these purposes; but as a result there was a corresponding loss of control over the money supply. The major innovation for the bond market following the introduction of competition and credit control was the ending of official price-stabilisation intervention for government bonds with more than one year to maturity. This implied giving lower priority to the maximisation of bond sales in favour of greater control of the money supply.

The instruments of debt management policy in Britain, apart from the now relegated open market operations and the conventional issues and redemptions of stock, include the operation by the Bank of England Capital Issues Committee of a queuing system for local authority and private sector bond issues which influences not only the volume but also the maturity of the stocks. Also, the differential tax treatment for central government bonds, as opposed to those of local authorities and the private sector, is used to influence demand for gilt-edged issues. The fact that British government bonds are exempt from capital gains tax means that they stand at a higher price than they otherwise would (assuming that the price of the bond stands below redemption price), although it does not necessarily reduce the cost of borrowing because the Exchequer no longer receives the tax receipts from this source. Thirdly, the authorities can influence demand by requiring certain types of lenders to hold a minimum proportion of specific categories of bonds. For instance, until July 1973 the discount houses were obliged to hold at least half their borrowed funds in public sector debt.

We now seek to compare the debt management policies of the Continental members of the EEC, as currently practised. A number of problems present themselves. The very term 'debt management' means different things to different monetary authorities, the root of the differences lying in the uneasy distinction between debt management and monetary policy. The objectives of their policies in relation to the bond markets are not always explicit and tend to change over time. Furthermore the instruments of these policies cannot be assessed exclusively in terms of the formal regulations since, on the one hand, the authorities may not make full use of their powers, and on the other they may additionally employ moral suasion. Finally, the instruments that may be employed in an emergency (however that is defined) may be very much more extensive than those in common use. These caveats must be borne in mind in reading Table 9 which summarises the present policy objectives of the Continental members of the EEC.

TABLE 9   Objectives of debt policy in continental countries of the EEC

	Belgium	France	Germany	Italy	Netherlands
Influence over slope and position of yield curve	x	x	x	x	x
Short-term stabilisation of bond prices	x		x	x	x
Priority for public sector borrowing	x	x		x	
Priority for domestic over foreign issues on domestic capital market	x	x		x	x
Debt service cost limitation	x	x		x	x

In Table 10 are set out the principal instruments commonly used in these countries to attain their objectives.

TABLE 10

Instruments of debt policy in Continental countries of the EEC

	Belgium	France	Germany	Italy	Netherlands
Open market operations in short & long-dated bonds	x		x	x	
Operation of bond issue timetable by public authorities	x			x	
Co-ordination of issues between public authorities and banks		x	x		x
Limitations on investment scope of financial intermediaries in favour of government bond issues	x	x		x	
Restrictions on access of foreign issuers to domestic bond market	x	x		x	x
Bond market regulation concentrates mainly on demand for capital	x	x			x

Official intervention on the bond market is probably least pervasive in Germany. The more liberal approach there and in the Netherlands is reflected in the scope available to private sector borrowers to make private placings of bonds without seeking prior approval from the authorities.

We now come to the central argument of this section: the need for the co-ordination of debt management policies as monetary union is approached. It was recognised by the Werner Report and has been succinctly demonstrated by Corden[15] that monetary union, if it is to be permanent and effective, needs to be accompanied by the transfer from the individual member countries to the Community of the right to create money. Were the separate countries to retain the power of money creation, each central bank would be in a position to engage in as much credit creation as it wished, regardless of the monetary policies of other member countries and the overall monetary position in the Community. The deficits of prodigal governments would have to be financed by the surpluses of the financially orthodox if monetary equilibrium were to be maintained. Unified control is the only workable long-term solution.

The case for the co-ordination of debt management policies of the member countries follows a similar line of reasoning. The present regime of exchange controls and exchange rate flexibility produces a different yield curve in each of the EEC countries. Monetary union, however, implies a unique yield curve in the Community. With monetary union, action taken by the authorities in each country in the field of debt would influence the Community yield curve, rather than just the domestic yield curve as is largely the case at present. On the other hand, for a given sale or purchase of bonds in the open market by one country there will be a much smaller impact on the Community yield curve than there would have been on the yield curve of the country concerned before monetary union.

Assume that each country is permitted to vary the size and maturity composition of its debt (as narrowly defined) although it has yielded the right to vary the monetary base. Some of the objectives that constrained its action prior to full convertibility and exchange rate rigidity no longer apply. For example, the general level of interest rates in the EEC would be greatly affected by a large-scale switch from taxation to bond issues as a source of exchequer financing in one country alone. And even if they were, other member countries might be expected to exercise compensating restraint on bond issues in the interests of the Community's general policy of economic stabilisation. If all countries ignored the consequences for the Community of their actions the results would be disastrous.

We have assumed that the money supply is controlled by the EEC central bank, which would prevent the straight monetisation of its debt by one country. On the other hand, one country, given the slope of the yield curve and given its expectations about the course of interest rates in the future, could rearrange the maturity composition of its debt so as to minimise its expected future debt service costs. If, for example, the Community yield curve was upward-sloping, that is, long-dated stocks were offering a higher return than short-dated, one country could reduce its interest costs, assuming certain conditions were satisfied, by substituting short- for long-dated stocks. Such action would require other member countries to step in to offset the impact of this rearrangement of the member country's debt (at a cost to themselves) in order to restore the original pattern of interest rates.

A revealing parallel to the situation that will arise in the EEC is the position in which local authorities find themselves in a single country. In the United Kingdom, for example, the monetary authorities place restrictions on the extent and form of local authority borrowing so as to ensure that their financing does not run counter to official policy.

These restrictions take the form of a queuing system for local authorities wishing to make bond issues and a requirement that no more than 20 per cent of all borrowing is in the form of short-term debt. In addition, overseas borrowing must receive Treasury approval in view of its impact on the balance of payments. Local authority activity in the bond market is confined to the provision of finance for expenditure programmes in the locality. Long-run cost minimisation within the constraints laid down by the monetary authorities is the sole objective of the borrowing arrangements of a local authority. Other considerations, such as economic stabilisation at the national level, are absent from the local authority's set of objectives and, because of the degree of capital mobility within the economy, regional economic stabilisation through the management of its debt is out of the question. The central government, on the other hand, has the full set of budgetary and stabilisation objectives to consider.

A number of lessons can be drawn from this comparison. With monetary union the Community authorities will be obliged to control not only the money supply in the EEC but also the size and maturity composition of the debt issued by the member countries. Only if this is done can there be a monetary policy at Community level that is not undermined by independent manipulation of their debt by member countries. Observe what follows from this. The size of each member government's issue of new debt, whether monetary or funded, is determined by the EEC central authorities in each period and, since the size of the debt issue in each country depends directly and exclusively on the budget deficit or surplus, it follows that member governments will no longer be able to exercise autonomy in determining their own budget balances. The total magnitude of each budget will still be decided by the government concerned. Even here, however, since the Treaty of Rome and the Commission itself are strong on rules to ensure competitive markets, only certain of each country's taxes will be available for independent variation, and therefore, freedom to determine the budget's size will be severely limited.

The economic stabilisation role of debt management will be transferred from the authorities in the member countries to the centre, leaving the former to finance their deficits at minimum cost within the constraints imposed by the Community. A queuing system will presumably be operated, the objective of which will be to ensure, first, that the desired proportions of net new Community issues and new member government issues are achieved and, secondly, that each member country gets an appropriate share. 'Net' here is used to distinguish between an issue that replaces an existing bond that has been redeemed and an entirely new issue that increases the size of the outstanding debt. Members will also be obliged to maintain a specified proportion of debt in each of the maturity categories. This may require quite an active debt management policy since long-dated bonds become medium-dated bonds, 'mediums' become 'shorts' and 'shorts' mature. Undated issues alone do not change category.

Vetting and approval will be needed for issues by member governments of bonds on markets outside the Community, since they will have an impact on the balance of payments between the EEC and the rest of the world. Of course, local authority and other public and corporate sector bond issues will fall within the scope of Community rather than national supervision. The rationing of access to the market and other constraints will need to be put on a basis that ensures equity, on the one hand among member countries and, on the other, among local authorities in the various countries, unless of course financing is to be part of the programme of regional redistribution.

We now turn to the positive rather than the defensive role of Community debt management policy. As part of its overall stabilisation strategy the EEC central bank will seek as far as it is able to determine the pattern of interest rates ruling in the union at any moment. The nature of the other targets and of the instruments adopted to secure them will depend largely on the manner in which integration has evolved. They will depend, for example, on the demands that are being made on the bond market as a source of revenue for the Community budget and the budgets of the member countries. Projections of the size of the European budget suggest that by 1980 it will be between 2 and 3 per cent of Community GNP.[16] Although it will undoubtedly increase as (or if) the EEC develops political will and cohesion, this appears a very small proportion, especially in view of the importance of central compared to local authority budgets in the United Kingdom and elsewhere. Although there has been a good deal of debate about the most suitable tax sources for the Euro-budget, little mention has been made of the alternative or additional source, namely bond financing. Bond finance would have, in fact, one great advantage over taxation in that it would avoid the problem of settling the proportion that each country should contribute.

Nevertheless, the fact remains that the Community demand will remain small relative to that of member countries and this will confer a strategic role upon the regulation of the queue for the bond market. Two important objectives of debt management for the central authorities in many countries are thus not directly applicable in the case of EEC debt management: (a) bond sales maximisation (except in so far as the Community seeks to adopt policies to encourage this on behalf of member governments); and (b) priority for central authority issues. Instead, one could foresee bond issues being used as an additional instrument of EEC regional policy.

Projects in the regions could be financed by bond finance rather than by taxation in the country concerned and queue-jumping or a larger allocation of bond issues in any given period would, in conjunction with EEC approval of the projects in question, permit them to proceed. Bond finance admittedly imposes a future obligation on the country in question to pay interest to non-residents and is thus a largely external debt in the same way that a bond issue by a local authority within a country constitutes a predominantly external debt. But depressed regions are unlikely to remain depressed for the duration of the loan's life and the bond issue would have enabled an inter-temporal transfer of consumption.

We have drawn attention earlier to the comparatively heavy reliance of Belgium and Italy on debt finance as a source of government revenue. This is going to present a problem of equity as monetary union approaches. Other countries will question why these two countries should have greater access to the bond market (greater in relation to the size of their domestic budgets) than the rest, unless preferential treatment is explicitly associated with regional policy. The difference between financing the budget by domestic taxation and financing it by debt is that the former associates a present benefit on the expenditure side with a present cost on the population, whereas the latter gives a present benefit but the cost is spread over the future. Italy and Belgium, if they were to be allowed to maintain their relatively higher demands on an integrated capital market, would be enjoying a rearrangement of their expenditure pattern over time, on a scale that was denied to others. It seems that both countries may have to prepare themselves for a greater dependence on domestic taxation in future.

The other special feature noted above was that central government debt in the United Kingdom is more or less equal to that of the rest of the member countries put together. This means that EEC monetary policy will have a more dramatic effect on the UK budget than on those of other countries. Existing debt, as it matures, has to be replaced with new debt, and the new debt has to be issued on a yield basis that reflects current monetary policy. In a period of tight monetary policy the debt becomes more expensive to service. There is no remedy here except for some concession to the United Kingdom when the debt pooling arrangements come to be made.

Capital Market Integration and the United Kingdom

There are two major effects of capital market integration upon the United Kingdom economy. The first is the impact on capital flows (direct, portfolio and other investment fund flows both to and from the other EEC countries and to and from non-EEC countries) and therefore, by extension, upon capital investment in the United Kingdom.[17] The second is the influence on the profits of financial intermediaries and the savings-investment process generally in the United Kingdom.

One of the conditions of Britain's entry into the EEC was that the UK government agreed to adjust its exchange control regulations so as to conform with the provisions of Community directives in relation to capital movements and to complete such adjustments over the transitional period of five years after accession. Each category of capital flow between the United Kingdom and the other EEC countries was allocated a terminal date by which it must be freed from exchange controls. Given the persistent balance-of-payments deficits, UK controls have traditionally been designed to deter outflows rather than inflows.[18] According to the programme UK outflows for direct investment in the EEC are to be freed from all controls by the end of 1974, for real estate purchase by June 1975 and for portfolio investment by the end of 1977. There is no certainty that conditions will be deemed appropriate for abiding by this timetable, and in any case the original Six members have already shown themselves capable of autonomous retrogressive action on capital controls. Having been almost completely liberalised well before the scheduled date, UK restrictions on direct investment were reimposed in the 1974 budget. Permission for such investments is now normally granted by the Bank of England so long as they are financed either with foreign currency borrowings or investment currency (under neither arrangement is there a loss to the balance of payments in the initial period). Official exchange will no longer be available unless the investment promises exceptionally large and rapid benefits to the balance of payments and meets the so-called 'super-criterion'.[19] That the authorities have thought it worthwhile to impose these new controls suggests that they will have some restrictive effect on capital outflows and thus their eventual removal may be expected to lead to an increase in outflows in this category.

United Kingdom residents wishing to use funds in this country to purchase EEC securities must also use investment currency, the centrepiece of the UK exchange control system.[20] Basically, if a UK resident wishes to use funds from this country to purchase foreign securities he must first obtain the necessary foreign exchange (or 'investment currency') from another UK resident disposing of foreign securities. It therefore follows that there will never be an outflow (or returning inflow for that matter) of portfolio investment funds in the UK balance of payments at least as far as UK residents are concerned. Any outflow or inflow would derive from foreign investors' portfolio investment activity in the UK, which does not go through this market. It also follows that if UK investors wish to hold foreign securities to a value greater than that of the foreign securities held in the pool when valued at ruling official exchange rates then a premium will develop on this investment currency. In fact the premium has been up to 60 per cent and down to 5 per cent in recent years and currently stands at 30 per cent. Since 1965 the 25 per cent surrender rule has been in operation, requiring 25 per cent of the proceeds of a sale of foreign securities to be converted at the official exchange rate while only 75 per cent is sold for the benefit of the premium. The effect is to reduce the pool of foreign exchange available for overseas security holdings and to improve the balance of payments by an amount that depends on the turnover of foreign securities per period. As an alternative to going through this market at all it is possible, subject to certain conditions and with the approval of the Bank of England, to invest in overseas securities financed by foreign borrowing.

By the end of 1977 at the latest according to the timetable, UK residents will no longer have to go through the investment currency market to purchase EEC securities. Now some £600 million or 10 per cent of the current £6,000 million pool of UK overseas portfolio investments is represented by EEC securities. The disappearance of the premium will mean a capital loss in excess of 20 per cent for current holders over the next three years. In the absence of changes to the present arrangements, increasing use will therefore be made of the foreign borrowing facility as a substitute for investment currency-financed holdings of EEC securities and this borrowing will probably be repaid to the detriment of the balance of payments sometime after the end of 1977. In the paper referred to above, three alternative methods of phasing out the control with respect to UK portfolio investment in the EEC are considered and the implication of each for the balance of payments is suggested. The approach that is most attractive on balance-of-payments grounds is to split the investment currency pools into two, one for EEC securities and the other for non-EEC securities. This division would permit the EEC investment currency premium to decline in response to market forces as the time of liberalisation approaches while that on non-EEC investment currency will reflect its own supply and demand conditions. Other things being equal this would leave the pool of investment currency for non-EEC security holdings at only £5,400 million rather than the present £6,000 million. Another advantage would be that the system could readily be converted into an intra-EEC two-tier exchange market for sterling while the extra-EEC investment currency market would dovetail smoothly into a common external fence of exchange control around the EEC.

Apart from the exchange controls there are also at present legal and administrative deterrents to UK portfolio investment in the EEC. As a matter of policy and often as a matter of law, pension funds and insurance companies in the United Kingdom are precluded from foreign security holdings; they are obliged to match the currency denomination of the investment with the currency of eventual liability. Such restrictions would disappear as capital markets in Europe became more integrated, though of course one would expect a similar relaxation for foreign intermediaries to produce a flow of funds in the opposite direction as well.

Inward investment in the UK is largely free of restrictions and those that exist are actually designed to encourage inflows. For example, non-EEC firms are not permitted to borrow sterling in order to undertake direct investment in this country. Foreign investors in the UK are also guaranteed complete repatriation rights and unlimited dividend distribution rights. No benefit to the balance of payments can therefore be expected on the inflows side to offset the outflows to the EEC that can be expected as controls relating to them are lifted.

Before UK entry into the EEC it was a common belief that one of the principal beneficiaries of UK membership would be the City. The financial expertise, the flexibility and resourcefulness of the UK institutions and the long experience gained in operating as an international financial centre was thought to ensure that London would quickly be able to assert its claim to be the financial capital of Europe. This optimism has now been tempered by a more careful appraisal of the situation.[21]

The UK has been able to develop its international business due in large measure to the relative freedom from control and restrictive regulation at home. Union with the EEC means that financial intermediaries throughout the Community will fall under a common set of regulations. It also means that exchange controls will take the form of a common fence around the Community, so potentially endangering London's non-EEC financial business. The City will therefore be competing on equal terms with financial intermediaries on the Continent for business both within and outside the EEC. Differences in relevant legal and fiscal aspects, in so far as any discretion remains for member countries in these respects, will be important in determining where multinational financial intermediaries set up and how large a share of the savings-investment process comes to London. Finally one must add that the City has been the subject of criticism at home on grounds such as those outlined in an earlier section. There has also been some resistance on the Continent to the intrusion of UK financial entrepreneurs.

References

1. G. Magnifico, *European Monetary Unification*, Macmillan, 1973; R.N. Cooper "Towards an International Capital Market?", in C.P. Kindleberger

and A. Shonfield (eds.), *North American and Western European Economic Policies*, Macmillan, 1971. There is also, of course, the painstaking Segré Report, *The Development of a European Capital Market*, European Economic Community Commission, Brussels, 1967.

2. G. Magnifico (op. cit., p. 24) has suggested that in a monetary union the size of the EEC, there may be a degree of compartmentalisation of regional capital markets such that interest rates may differ slightly from region to region and that a regionally discriminatory monetary policy may therefore be possible. To support this contention he quotes from the study of this issue in the United States context by W. Isard, "The Value of the Regional Approach in Economic Analysis" in National Bureau of Economic Research, *Regional Income*, Princeton University, Princeton, 1954.

3. Cf. R.N. Cooper, op. cit., and R.G. Hawkins in *International Mobility and Movement of Capital*, edited by F. Machlup and others, National Bureau of Economic Research, New York, 1972.

4. Not only has the subject of capital controls in the EEC escaped attention almost entirely in the literature, but there is remarkably little analytical empirical study in this area in general. Important contributions that have been made, however, include those by D.A. Snider, 'The Case for Capital Controls to Relieve the US Balance of Payments', *American Economic Review*, Vol. 54, June 1964; N.S. Fieleke, 'The Welfare Effects of Controls over Capital Exports from the United States', *Essays in International Finance* No. 82, Princeton University, International Finance Section, 1971; Sir Alec Cairncross, 'Control of Long-Term Capital Movements', Brookings Institution Staff Paper, 1973; and more specifically on one type of control, the dual rate system, J.M. Fleming *Essays in International Economics*, Allen and Unwin, 1971, Ch. 12.

5. We are considering specific capital controls here rather than extending the definition of control to include offsetting them domestically or financing them internationally.

6. Treaty of Rome, Article 67. Provisions in respect of capital markets are found in Articles 67-73.

7. In F. Machlup and others, op. cit.

8. See for example, J.M. Fleming, 'Dual Markets and other Remedies for Disruptive Capital Flows', IMF DM/73/61. The dual rate has the outstanding merit of promoting flows in one direction as much as it discourages them in the other.

9. See, for example, the comparative study in *The Future of London as an International Financial Centre*, HMSO, 1973.

10. On the Eurocurrency market see, for example, F. Machlup, 'Eurodollar Creation: a Mystery Story', *Banca Nazionale del Lavoro* Quarterly Review, September, 1970; A.K. Swoboda, 'Eurodollars and the World Money Supply: Implications and Control', in *Europe and the Evolution of the International Monetary System*, edited by A.K. Swoboda, Sijthoff, Leiden, 1973; and G. Bell, *The Eurodollar Market and the International Financial System*, Macmillan, 1973. On the Eurobond Market see J.F. Chown and R. Valentine, *The International Bond Market in the 1960s: its Development and Operation*, Praeger 1968; and M. Mendelson, 'The Eurobond and Capital Market Integration', *Journal of Finance*, March 1972.

11. See P.K. Woolley, 'The Economics of the United Kingdom Stock Exchange' *Moorgate and Wall Street*, Spring 1974.

12. See A. Singh, 'Take-overs: their Relevance to the Stock Market and the Theory of the Firm', Department of Applied Economics, Cambridge, Monograph 19, Cambridge University Press, 1971.
13. This section is based on an article entitled 'Debt Management in the EEC' that appeared in the *National Westminster Bank Review*, February 1974, under the joint authorship of J.H. Coates and the present writer.
14. 'Official transactions in the Gilt-edged Market', *Bank of England Quarterly Bulletin*, Vol. 6, No. 2, June 1966.
15. W.M. Corden; 'Monetary Integration', *Princeton Essays in International Finance*, No. 93, April 1972
16. See Chapter 7, pp. 102-3 below.
17. S.M. Yassukovich considered the impact of UK membership of the EEC on capital flows between the UK and the other member countries in his contribution to an earlier Federal Trust book: *The Economics of Europe*, edited by John Pinder, Charles Knight 1971.
18. For an up-to-date and detailed analysis of the UK system of exchange controls, past and present, see Sir Alec Cairncross, 'Control of Long-term International Capital Movements', Brookings Institute Staff Paper, 1973, Ch. 4.
19. A benefit to the UK balance of payments equal to the initial outflow within eighteen months and continuing thereafter.
20. See P.K. Woolley, 'The UK Investment Currency Premium', Lloyds Bank Review, July 1974 and 'Portfolio Theory and the UK Investment Currency Premium' forthcoming.
21. Valuable contributions to this debate have been made in J.E. Nash, 'The Future of Financial Centres in a European Monetary Union', published by Societe Universitaire Europeenne de Recherce Financiere, 1972, and *The Future of London as an International Financial Centre*, HMSO, 1973.

4 LABOUR MARKET POLICY

Santosh Mukherjee

There is much scope for confusion in the term 'social policy'. Free movement of workers from one member country to another[1] was, to the founders, a matter of rational allocation of (manpower) resources, quite unrelated to 'social' considerations. That men and women should have 'equal remuneration for the same work'[2] has the ring of a social issue, though in fact, or course, this stemmed from initial French worries about their potential cost disadvantage in intra-Community competition. No one with any political influence has bothered very much about removing the wage disparity between men and women. Little has changed and no revolutionary upheavals are in sight.

The Treaty-makers made one gesture of awareness of the costs that would bear on some individuals as a result of freeing the flow of goods and resources in the Community, embodied in Articles 123-7 setting out the terms of a European Social Fund. Since the reduction and ultimate removal of tariffs were bound to cause, or aggravate, structural unemployment, the Fund had to go about 'promoting within the Community employment facilities and the geographical and occupational mobility of workers.' Resources to be put to this purpose were, in the early years, derisory. During the first nine years of the Social Fund's life annual outlays averaged £3.5 million. Information about events since 1968 is given in Table 1. While the Table shows a rising expenditure up to 1971 the Fund still received rather less than 2 per cent of the cash passing through the Commission's hands. Even the 1972 allocation for the Fund, large by comparison with earlier years, was only 28 per cent of what the Commission spent that year on the cost of administration alone.

Social policy, then, was a matter of alleviating in a minor way the adverse repercussions on individuals which could be expected to occur as restraints to trade within the Six were gradually removed. But the scale on which this enterprise was conceived clearly implies a presumption that most of the necessary redeployment of manpower would take place through the normal allocative processes of the labour market. Only at the margin, it was thought, would there be need for some aid from national governments and the Community.

Since great store was set by the principle of free movement of

TABLE 2

ECSC Budget outlays on readaptation and all other activities (£ million) 1968-1972

Year	Outlays on readaptation	All ECSC expenditure (total levy budget)	Readaptation outlays as percentage of total expenditure	Number of workers assisted	Outlay per head (£s)
1968	5.4	14.9	36.0	42,748	125.83
1969	11.0	25.1	44.0	30,978	356.25
1970	10.5	22.5	46.7	21,747	482.92
1971	6.8	23.4	28.8	11,083	609.17
1972	6.4	25.7	24.8	18,190	350.42

Sources: General Reports of the ECSC and Activities of the Communities.

workers, foreseeable obstacles to this had to be removed by the Treaty. It was this object alone that brought the Treaty into the low politics of social security systems. To protect migrant workers and their dependants it was necessary to oblige member countries to honour social security entitlements built up by individuals in one country, when occasion arose for benefits to be paid out in another.[3] Here, the Treaty obligations were clear-cut.

Alignment of Social Security

In striking contrast were the Treaty's requirements[4] on general harmonisation of member countries' social security systems. Though the Commission has done a lot of study and education in this area, the Treaty obligations are such that member countries have not had to do anything unless they wanted to make changes, and in practice each country has just carried on with its own system.

Now, whether social security systems should or should not be aligned is controversial. If the principle is accepted, the discussion can centre on the extent to which that alignment should be taken. This consideration of common social security systems centres on two issues: the harmonisation of methods and whether or not the level of benefits should be allowed to continue to be different as between member countries.

A quick way of estimating the implications of moves towards harmonisation of levels of benefits is to look at the share of social security expenditure in total public spending in Britain. Financing social security took almost 18 per cent of total United Kingdom public expenditure in 1971. It was the biggest single item, costing nearly half as much again as the outlay on education. Britain's social security system is of course much more dependent on Exchequer finance than its counterparts in the other EEC countries; most Community members get the bulk of finance for social security through direct contributions by employer and employee, and this reduces Exchequer outlays on these schemes. This difference is a big practical difficulty in moving towards alignment of social security systems in the EEC.

Nevertheless it is more than likely that economic and monetary union will eventually compel alignment, if not full harmonisation, of methods of financing social security in each member country; the pace of this development will be governed by the speed of progress towards monetary union. Harmonisation of the level of payments to individuals under national social security programmes will take longer.

As things are now, there is no sign that member countries actively wish to take steps to align their social security schemes, whether methods of financing or levels of benefit. Social security schemes are even more complicated than tariff structures. Apart from the agonising technical difficulties of harmonising nine national systems of social security for the citizen, there is a still more daunting obstacle in the way of harmonisation, the transfer of funds between countries which would be necessary if levels of social security benefits were made identical in the Community as a whole.

There are great disparities in the total outlay on social security from country to country in the EEC; and benefits per head differ widely. United Kingdom expenditure in 1971-2 was about £4600 million; over the same period, and in respect of a comparable range of contingencies, expenditure in Germany was something over £10,000 million.

How much a country chooses to spend on maintaining the income of citizens, such as the unemployed or those in retirement, is a matter of political choice. Recipients of social security benefits are not as well organised as a political pressure group like the farmers, whether in Britain or elsewhere in the EEC.

A common social security policy for parity of income maintenance benefits in each country would require Community budgetary provision of at least four to six times the funds now going to financing the CAP. Moreover, the necessary transfers from one country to another would be larger than in the CAP. There would have to be very compelling reasons for national governments to agree to contribute on this scale to the Community budget.

When economic and monetary union reaches the stage where the domestic economies of the Nine are as interdependent as different regions are at present within individual countries, harmonisation of both methods and benefit levels of social security will become unavoidable. The need will become compelling as much on grounds of avoidance of distortion of competition as on wider considerations of social equity. There is room for a variety of opinion about how soon this will come about, or whether, indeed, it will ever be quite as compelling a need as is suggested here. What can be agreed is that there are as yet no powerful forces, despite the Summit agreement in 1972, propelling member countries in the direction of the kind of harmonisation of social security systems that would lead to big changes in the Community budget.

Wider Social Issues

The Treaty of Rome was largely irrelevant to the longer-term issues of social policy. There was not even a procedural framework within which social issues such as the alignment of social security schemes could be considered within the Community. Up to a point, this deficiency was remedied by the 1972 Summit agreement, but this made progress only in procedural terms, and conceptual difficulties remain in discussions of common social programmes.

The functions initially envisaged for the Social Fund were a rudimentary and grudging acknowledgement of the need for an ambulance service for damage to a minority of individuals; social policy issues in the Community of the Nine during the 1970s are quite different from these objectives. Social policy issues now concern counteracting pollution, increasing individual participation in political and industrial decision-making; moderating the harmful effects of industrial development on the quality of life. These are exciting but wider and less tangible matters than the adaptation of workpeople to new jobs when their old employment disappears because of altered product demand; or, the process of regenerating regions blighted by the decline of traditional industries.

Though the division has to be pretty rough and ready, it is possible to distinguish those 'social' issues that are largely and directly centred on employment and others that are not. The contingencies covered by social security systems are divisible, broadly speaking, into those related to giving people an income when they are unemployed, and income maintenance for all other contingencies (retirement pensions, family allowances and so on).

By narrowing the focus to unemployment, manageable and practical directions of common policy can be opened up. Income maintenance during unemployment takes a relatively small proportion of total outlays on social security, and harmonisation of this sector would be less costly in transfers of funds between members of the Community, and involve less expansion of the EEC budget than a programme of across-the-board harmonisation of social security systems. On grounds of Community precedents, and more importantly the logic of economic union, there are sound reasons for making a start on a common policy for dealing with unemployment. This approach occupies the middle ground between the impoverished view of social policy embodied in the original Social Fund, and the current vogue issues exemplified by anti-pollution and pro-participation campaigns.

Community Labour Market Policy

In operating the ECSC, the High Authority put a big part of its total effort into dealing with unemployment. Though the full ramifications of the ECSC's activity in this field cannot be shown simply by the accounts these are nevertheless a striking indicator. Table 2 shows that

TABLE 1

EEC Budget allocations by (some) areas of activity 1968 to 1971 (£ million)

Activity	1968	1969	1970	1971[1]	1972
1. European Parliament	3.4	3.7	4.3	na	na
2. Council of Ministers	3.8	4.1	4.8	na	na
3. Court of Justice	0.8	0.8	0.9	na	na
4. Administration	36.6	40.7	42.5	62.0	155.8
5. Agricultural Fund	852.1	1062.3	1270.5	1096.0	1456.0
6. Social Fund	10.2	13.9	17.5	23.0	43.8
7. Commission total (4-6)	898.9	1116.9	1330.5	1181.0	1655.6
8. Food Aid	–	–	6.9	8.0	15.3
9. Grand totals (1-6 and 8)	906.9	1125.5	1337.4	–	–

Notes and sources: 1 Estimated: not strictly comparable with amounts for 1968-70.
General Reports of the Activities of the Communities, for 1968, 1969 and 1970.
The United Kingdom and the European Communities, Cmnd. 4715, July 1971.

from 1968 to 1970 some 36-47 per cent of the ECSC's income from levy was put to readapting or redeploying workpeople who would otherwise have become unemployed. In 1971 and 1972 this activity took a smaller proportion of ECSC levy revenue, because there were fewer workers affected by closures and contractions of activity in those years, though even then some 25-29 per cent of the levy was spent on adaptation. For the EEC analogous activities attracted less than 1.5 per cent of the total budget during 1968-70, with a rise to 2-2.6 per cent in the two subsequent years.

ECSC cash outlays for each individual helped in this way varied from £126 in 1968 to £609 in 1971. These sums were matched by expenditures of equal amounts by national authorities. Consequently, in 1971 the average assistance given to the individual under the ECSC scheme was £1218.[5]

Redundant workpeople in the case of the ECSC were more fortunate than their peers in other sectors within the EEC. Expenditure on redeployment for every person helped by the Social Fund was, in 1971, running at about one-third of the rate of outlay in the ECSC. Social Fund resources are scheduled to rise, at some as yet unspecified time, to £100 million annually. When that happens, allowing for inflation and aiming at the ECSC level of assistance, the Fund will be able to come to the aid of some 125,000 people each year. Adding in the obligation on national authorities to match outlays from the Social Fund, the individual who has stumbled in the labour market will have the possibility, at some date in the future, of total assistance approaching £1600 contributed jointly by the Community and his own national government.

It was only in May 1972 that the Social Fund was enlarged, with a more flexible set of rules about its role. As it took the Commission something over three years of hard labour to achieve that, it may seem ungracious to cavil so soon at this outcome. Yet, in reforming the Fund much was borrowed from the ECSC experience in facilitating redeployment. One fundamental element of the ECSC activity on redeployment has been its comprehensive coverage. Of course, it was easier for the High Authority to adopt that approach as it had in its care only the workpeople in coal and steel, a much more manageable number than the total employed labour force in the whole Community, for which the Social Fund has, in principle, to cater.

What would be involved in applying the ECSC type programme for redeployment in the Community generally? In budgetary terms the implications are substantial. There are no official figures about the number of individuals who lose their jobs in the Nine each year through redundancy. For Britain, France and Germany a figure of 1,000,000 annually for each country is probably not too wide of the mark. The other Six, taken together, have perhaps an annual redundancy rate of 750,000. A rough total, then, for the Community's annual rate of redundancy is 3,750,000. To provide aid to all of these people on the scale envisaged in the enlarged Social Fund (£800 per head) would cost £3,000 million (say, 7,200 million u.a.). That amount is rather more than double the whole of current Community budgetary resources for all expenditures, and of the present Community budget £1,300 million (about 3,100 million u.a.) is spent on the Agricultural Guidance and Guarantee Fund.

At first sight, then, full coverage even only of redundancy by the Social Fund needs a forbiddingly large amount of money. And presumably the present requirement would be maintained that national governments should match £ for £ all expenditure of this kind made from the central Community budget. Yet, even on those assumptions, total outlays per head on individuals in need of aid for redeployment will be only about £1,600. Since the analogy is with the type of activity in the ECSC, that sum of money would have to be stretched to cover income maintenance for the individual, costs of retraining, relocation costs and topping up of wages for a limited period in the new job to which the individual has to move. How much of the total goes on each one of these items is determined by the particular circumstances of the individual. But overall, given the range of assistance to be encompassed, an average redeployment cost of £800 from the Community matched by a like sum from the national governments would not be excessively generous.

Changes in the structure of employment are particularly large in regions with older industries which are in decline because of changes in the demand for their products. The prospect of spending £3,000 million on redeployment of manpower is less forbidding if it is recognised that some proportion of this total should be regarded as a contribution to Community regional policy.

Regional aid, whether at national or at Community level, goes to infrastructure development, the conversion of existing fixed capital or the building of new plant, machinery and equipment and, finally, for the readaptation of manpower to new activities. Britain and Italy, with the biggest regional development programmes, have tended to put practically all aid into infrastructure and physical capital, largely ignoring the need for investment in the conversion of manpower.

There is a danger that an enlarged Community regional policy will have a similar bias built into it. A pertinent question at this stage is, therefore, whether the functional divisions in the Commission and the Directorates are right. Arguably, a more relevant structure would be a Commissioner and Directorate for Employment with responsibility for both regional development and manpower redeployment. The

Directorate and Commissioner for Social Affairs could then get on with the more nebulous but immensely important industrial issues of participation, the organisation and responsibilities of companies, and, on a wider front, issues of income distribution as well as the whole range of questions including education, social security and the protection of the environment, which are involved in improving the quality of life. Though the major items of social security would logically form a part of this complex of issues, the system of maintenance for workers who are unemployed can equally logically be detached from it and made part of the Employment and Manpower Redeployment function.

Table 3 shows the amount of unemployment in the enlarged Community. As the basis of compilation of national statistics varies from country to country the figures are not wholly reliable, but a number of broad points can be made. In the present Nine taken together, unemployment as a percentage of all employees averages about 3 per cent. Even allowing for the difference in size of each country's labour force, the incidence of unemployment is not evenly distributed. Italy's is the largest share; Britain with between 25 and 32 per cent of the Community total also contrasts with France or Germany, both of which have much lower levels of unemployment.

In each country, unemployment is unevenly distributed among regions. Those parts of countries most in need of aid for regional development are also the greatest centres of unemployment. Consequently, it is plausible to maintain that the adaptation of manpower for redeployment, grants of assistance for both infrastructure and capital growth, as much as income maintenance for the unemployed, provide a continuum of activities all related to micro-level policy for employment. Community (common) policies already exist, or are in the making, for both manpower adaptation and regional development. There remains the question of the need for and feasibility of an EEC common policy on income maintenance in unemployment.

International comparisons of social security can be misleading, but on the narrow question of benefits to people who are unemployed, reasonable comparisons are possible. In 1970, with about 175,000 people unemployed, Germany spent some £90 million on their income maintenance; British expenditure in the same year was £159 million for an unemployment register carrying about 658,000. Danish, Belgian and French levels of benefit are also quite considerably higher than in Britain.

A Community policy on unemployment benefits could be a positive instrument for encouraging changes in the structure of employment. Often, and increasingly, Community countries have simultaneously both a significant amount of unemployment and a substantial number of unfilled job vacancies. National labour markets left to themselves are

64

TABLE 3

Number of people registered as unemployed by National Public
Employment Services of the Nine (1970-72)

	1970	1971	1972[1]
Belgium (December)	87,200	99,000	76,700
Germany (December)	175,100	269,800	375,100
France (November)	375,000	521,000	417,000
Italy (November)	973,900	1,056,000	1,168,300
Luxembourg (December)	33	22	28
Netherlands (December)	66,600	114,500	134,300
"Old" Community	1,677,833	2,060,322	2,171,428
United Kingdom (December)	657,845	996,892	781,630
Denmark[2]	24,115	24,500	24,500
Ireland (December)	62,998	71,354	71,346
3 new Members	744,958	1,092,746	877,476
Enlarged Community	2,422,791	3,153,068	3,048,904

Notes: [1] January for all except UK – December; and Denmark – estimated
annual average.

[2] Estimated.

unable to match demand for manpower with the available supply.

Demand for labour in the tertiary sector continues to grow strongly, originating to a substantial extent from public sector activity in education, health and other community and welfare services. With Denmark as the one exception, wages in tertiary employment are much lower than wages in manufacturing industry. One reason for the coexistence of high unemployment and many vacancies is that individuals hang on, supported by unemployment benefits, in the hope of being able to return to a job with pay and conditions resembling the one that has disappeared. Another important barrier to inter-sectoral mobility is the lack of vocational skills and of opportunities to acquire them. This phenomenon is in turn frequently involved with complex sociological difficulties about class and status. The sociological difficulties are least tractable, and common EEC policies should be devised for influencing the other two factors causing inefficiencies in labour markets.

The aim of a common EEC labour market policy would be, to take an extreme example, to enable a steel worker whose services were no longer needed by the British Steel Corporation to become a hospital ancillary worker. The purpose of policy would be to make that change possible without too much of the cost being put on the man who goes through this socially advantageous transformation. What has just been said exposes the complexity and difficulties with which a common policy for transforming the structure of employment would have to contend. Yet, something close to this has been done for coal and steel workers by the ECSC for many years. In Britain, too, similar arrangements have existed for some time for coal miners, and negotiations are now taking place between the British Steel Corporation and the Commission for improved schemes of 'tide-over' pay which would make up the redeployed steel worker's wages to 90 per cent of his previous earnings for a period of up to three years in his new job. 'Tide-over' payments are temporary wage subsidies to ease the individual's transition from a high wage occupation to one with lower pay. While this need not necessarily involve a move between sectors, a Community policy could deliberately use this wage subsidy to increase manpower supply to tertiary (public service) vacancies which now remain unfilled through the normal functioning of free labour markets.

Individuals in transit between sectors with different wage levels will, in all probability, need spells of conversion training. Community policy on training for skill conversion to aid inter-sectoral mobility could be founded on the most advanced models, such as those in France and Germany, already available in member countries. Wider provision of retraining, interlocked with schemes for tide-over payments in the newer jobs, could become the basis for a significantly new approach to the treatment of unemployment.

A passive approach, where the state provides high (in Denmark) or minimal (as in Britain) income maintenance to individuals who are without jobs can be transformed in interrelationship with measures for regional regeneration and the active redeployment of manpower. With some three million unemployed in 1972, the governments of the Nine, taken together, were paying out about £750-£800 million in income maintenance for people without jobs. That was wholly passive expenditure. With a Social Fund having the resources proposed earlier in this paper, current member government expenditure on unemployment benefit could be channelled partly to retraining and in part to tide-over wage subsidy.

All of this implies large administrative structures, but each of the Nine, except Italy, have well-established public employment services. These institutions have long experience of administration of unemployment benefit, and in most cases they have also run retraining schemes. Once the principles of a dynamic redeployment policy based on retraining and temporary, degressive, wage subsidisation are accepted, the existing national public employment services could be adapted to administering that kind of scheme rather than the payment of unemployment benefits. The administrative cost of this change need not necessarily be any greater than present outlays on existing government institutions for supporting national labour markets.

As we saw earlier, to give ECSC standard aid to everyone likely to need redeployment assistance in the enlarged Community would mean a Social Fund budget of £3,000 million, matched by a direct outlay of £3,000 million by national governments. Of the latter sum, perhaps half can be found from a straight transfer of present national outlays on income support to the unemployed and on the retraining schemes for adaptation to new employment. Even allowing for that, no less than £4,500 million of new money, two-thirds for the Community's budget and the remaining one-third as additional national outlays, would be involved in the finance of an adequate programme of active manpower policy for the Nine.

References

1. Articles 48, 49 and Directives and Regulations.
2. Article 119.
3. Article 51 and Regulations.
4. Mostly in Article 118.
5. These figures understate actual ECSC outlays for redeployment in that they leave out of account ECSC loans to help finance new jobs for coal and steel workers in other sectors. By 1971, these loans amounted in all to £450-500 million.

5 REGIONAL PROBLEMS AND POLICY

A. Monetary Union and Regional Economies

Geoffrey Denton

The links between international economies and regional economies have always been close, the optimum currency area has been defined as a region, and the problem for economic and monetary union 'reduces to whether or not western Europe can be considered a single region'.[1] Attention to the question of feasibility, however, produces a rather different definition. The consensus view appears to be that in order to adopt a single currency an area need only satisfy either one of two criteria: first, that there should be internal factor mobility (but external factor immobility); and secondly, that there should not be a high degree of wage/price interdependence with other regions. This two-fold definition establishes the conditions in which parity change as an adjustment policy is, respectively, either unnecessary or ineffective. The regional problem in the context of monetary union appears to consist in the second criterion being either already met as a result of autonomous integration (an empirical question which is surrounded by much confusion and little convincing evidence) or in process of being created (by deliberate policies under the Werner or other schemes); while the first criterion is not fully met. Parity changes may become ineffective or be made impossible, while factor mobility within the area remains far from perfect.

The definition of regions is crucial to the assessment of the effects of monetary integration. In this chapter we distinguish two kinds of region in addition to the Mundellian single currency area of the Community as a whole. *National regions* are the existing member states which are assumed to become a new form of economic region within the monetary union. Although they will lose the distinctive characteristic of the Mundellian region, the possibility of parity change, there are, and will remain, structural and institutional differences among these existing national economies. Their governments will retain substantial powers to make their own economic policy even within a monetary union, and their frontiers are likely to continue to represent obstacles to factor mobility, despite policies designed to increase cross-frontier mobility. *Sub-regions* are the existing regions within the various member states, which though not Mundellian regions have problems regarding the external mobility of factors which give rise to persistent economic and social differences.

The existence of the sub-regions is recognised by the member states and was formally accepted by the European Community from the beginning. Following the proposals for monetary union it is the problems of sub-regions to which most regional policy discussions, both official and unofficial, have been addressed. The political situation regarding the national regions, however, does not appear to correspond to their forthcoming economic status, and the question how the existing national economies will be affected by their new status as national regions has therefore been inadequately examined. The Thomson Report[2] appeared somewhat contradictory on the issue. First it stated that:

it should be emphasised that the Community is here concerned with problems linked to certain limited geographical areas. For it is not the role of Community regional policy to act as an overall corrective to all economic problems affecting the growth rate of a member state. (pp. 8-9)

The exaggeration 'all economic problems' here camouflages the important national-regional consequences which Community regional policy should be prepared to tackle. Later, the Report discussed the use of the European Regional Fund, and stated that this must be 'used in a manner quite independent of any criterion of *juste retour,* to tackle (sub-) regional problems according to their size and urgency.' (p.14) Although the distinction between national and sub-regions is useful for the purpose of analysis, the economic growth of a national region cannot in practice be dissociated from the progress of its component sub-regions. And if Community funds are to be directed to the more urgent and significant regional problems, judged by Community-wide criteria, the possibility of inter-national-regional transfers (that is, transfers among the member states) arising out of Community sub-regional aids must be left open.

It is thus superfluous to argue whether or not Community funds should give regional aid to member states. If sub-regions are to be given effective aids not based on *juste retour,* national regions will *ipso facto* have to receive transfers. This effect is quite transparent in the general acceptance that the Community Fund, while it may directly finance its own programmes in areas of special common interest, such as cross-border regions, will normally work indirectly by financing national programmes of aid to sub-regions.[3] Since sub-regional aids will continue to be financed largely from national funds, the possibility is left open that national governments could diminish national financing in line with the growth of Community financing. No doubt this would be contrary to Community policy, but unless done blatantly it would be impossible to police. Community sub-regional aids could thus in practice be indistinguishable from Community subventions to member states. But even if ear-marking were carried out so successfully that Community aids were to represent a net addition to total aids to a sub-region, economic interdependence of the sub-regions with their national regions could result in the leakage of much of the aid. Community checks on the type of activity eligible for Community-financed assistance could be nullified by the switch of nationally-financed programmes towards projects with high spill-overs outside the sub-regions.

The exclusive emphasis on sub-regions is therefore likely to make the promises extracted by the British from the October 1972 Summit Meeting uncashable. While the Commission in 1973 accepted the greater part of the British map of problem regions, *juste retour* is already enshrined in the acceptance also of the regional maps of the other members. While the final outcome cannot be predicted in advance of agreement on setting up the fund and on the criteria and the details of implementation, it seems likely that national rather than Community-wide criteria are likely to emerge from the horse-trading about aids to sub-regions in the absence of an overt commitment to the principle of inter-member state transfers. What the maps and the criteria do not achieve in the emasculation of Community regional policy, the likely inadequate size of the regional fund to generate substantial transfers among member states will complete.

In addition to the worries about the future of the British national region which arise from this discussion, there is further cause for concern about the future of existing nationally-financed aids to sub-regions. The Competition Directorate has made substantial progress in recent years by achieving acceptance of the practice of Community control over national subsidies to sub-regions. From the point of view of maintaining undistorted conditions for trade among the members this development is to be welcomed, for there is increasing recognition that even general regional aids, through their sectoral effects, may frequently distort international trade in individual commodities.[4] But the important point is that controls of such regional aids may delay the solution of regional problems. While a devaluation continues to be available as an instrument for providing a general increase in the competitiveness of sub-regions *vis-a-vis* other national economies, controls on regional aids suspected of creating specific distortions to trade may be acceptable to domestic policy-makers. In the absence of this adjustment policy the development of further controls on national programmes of sub-regional aids would be more serious.

All these problems may be regarded as lacking urgency if it is considered impossible that a full monetary union would be implemented and maintained without further development of Community policy in a sense favourable both to national and to sub-regions. A really large Community Regional Fund, aiding sub-regions defined according to Community criteria, including the whole of a member state if this should fall entirely within the definition, and generating substantial net transfers to national economies with a high incidence of regional problems, would constitute a sufficient expression of Community solidarity on the regional issues to allow progress with monetary integration. The situation could become more urgent, however, if monetary integration were accelerated by either a rapid autonomous growth of economic interdependence (for example, through trade union federations equalising real wages through the Community), or a too rapid progress on the side of monetary institutions and policy. In this respect the imaginative **Europa** proposal, with its risk that the new currency might possibly drive out national currencies too rapidly, is perhaps more dangerous than the cumbersome and ineffective Werner processes.

The Adjustment of Disequilibrium Among National Regions
If the Werner proposals were enacted with respect to 'locking' the individual parities, the national regions would experience significant changes in the nature of their internal payments disequilibria and the appropriate adjustment policies arising out of the removal of the parity adjustment mechanism for maintaining competitiveness.

Equalisation of factor earnings is likely to take the form of an upward alignment of earnings to the level prevailing in the most prosperous region of the union, especially if transnational trade unions have been formed. As a result the competitive position of the less prosperous, relatively inefficient, low-investment, low-wage, national regions will tend to be undermined. Whereas these less productive regions would previously have been able to remain competitive with the help of successive currency devaluations, in a monetary union their competitive positions would be progressively eroded, and unless they could regain a competitive advantage for some of their export goods by raising efficiency, they would tend to face persistent trade deficits.

A national region which was in overall deficit, with the deficit arising in its trade within the Community, would not be able to devalue but would have to correct the deficit in the short term by a reduction of internal aggregate demand, and in the long term by lowering its relative price level. Since factor prices could not be reduced, the latter could only be achieved by raising productivity or by cutting back high-cost activities. Increasing productivity would presumably be difficult on account of all the reasons why the national region had low productivity in the first place. In both the short and the long term, then, reduction of output and employment are likely. Similarly, a national region experiencing a trade surplus would face some pressure to resort to increasing its internal expenditure and raising its relative price level, though the major burden of adjustment, as in the international balance-of-payments case, is likely to rest on the deficit region.

The significance for adjustment policy of the removal of parity changes as an adjustment mechanism depends in part on the proportion of GNP traded. In general, the smaller the proportion of GNP traded, the greater would be the preference for parity adjustments over domestic demand management in response to external deficit. Thus, monetary union would have the most serious consequences for countries such as the United Kingdom, with a relatively low degree of trade interdependence with the other members.

Regional Effects of Common Parity Changes

It is not necessary for each member individually to balance its payments with respect to extra-trade; a deficit on the external payments of a member could in principle be offset by other members' external surpluses together with a surplus in intra-transactions between the member and the rest of the monetary union. However, the interesting case is that of the member who is in overall payments deficit, with a significant part of the deficit arising from its extra-trade, while other members and the Community as a whole are in surplus externally. In this situation a devaluation of the external parity of the common currency is not called for, since it would only increase the existing overall surplus between the monetary union and third countries. The common currency will thus represent a compromise between the different economic requirements of the various national regions, and the final value of the common currency *vis-a-vis* gold and/or the dollar will be a mean of the parities of the present separate national currencies.

A probable consequence of this compromise would be that fast-growing national regions with strong trade and payments positions, such as Germany, would have an 'undervalued' currency at their disposal for trade with third countries, while slower-growing national regions like the United Kingdom would have the additional disadvantage of having to use an 'overvalued' currency for such trade. Thus, for example, Germany would be better able to resist competition from Japanese imports with the help of an 'undervaluation effect' of the monetary union on the erstwhile DM; while the United Kingdom would be less able to face this competition given an overvaluation effect on the erstwhile £ sterling.

The use of exchange-rate adjustments in the face of national extra-payments imbalance would thus also be effectively removed from the range of possible economic policy instruments. (Though there would be some consolation in that an externally-oriented member would find domestic deflation a less costly adjustment policy for extra-trade imbalance than would internally-oriented members.) The implications of this effect of monetary union are, of course, familiar with respect to the existing sub-regions, which are already unable to produce regional devaluations or revaluations, at least by normal policy means; the value of the £ sterling is not adjusted solely on account of the problems of the Scottish economy.

Different national regions may also continue to experience different national propensities to inflate within the monetary union since the causes of differential rates of inflation are unlikely to be closely aligned in the foreseeable future.[5] The existence of different propensities to inflate implies the presence of different trade-offs between unemployment and price inflation, and this will cause major problems for any attempts at policy co-ordination both in the short and the medium term. More important for present purposes, those national regions which have experienced relatively high rates of inflation, for example, the United Kingdom, would tend to suffer progressive competitive disadvantages compared with those national regions, such as Germany, which have had less inflation, in view of their inability to devalue to compensate for the unfavourable cost structures which the high rates of inflation will bring about.

Corrective action by the uncompetitive national region in the form of deflationary measures would be costly in terms of loss of output and employment since the imbalance now under discussion is long-term persistent and not the short-term imbalance for which deflation can sometimes be a more plausible alternative to devaluation. Moreover, in the light of experience in various countries in the early 1970s, it is by no means obvious that *any* conceivable degree of deflation can adjust fundamental differences in cost structures. Attempts to solve a structural payments deficit by deflation might merely create higher levels of unemployment with little or no change in the rate of inflation. Moreover, the inflation could even be accelerated by the deflation slowing down the rate of growth of overall productivity. Productivity may rise rapidly in individual industries under deflationary conditions, but if labour is released merely to add to the pool of unemployed, there need be no increase in overall national productivity. The cost-push effects of increased taxes, and a general increase in trade union militancy in these conditions, could indeed make the inflation even more intractable, as in the United Kingdom in the early 1970s. The deflation is at the same time likely to reduce the incentive to invest. Thus the national regional problem could be aggravated.

If the socio-economic determinants of inflation are thus unamenable to correction by means of deflation, the removal in a monetary union of the possibility of adjustment via periodic devaluations is indeed serious.

Would a monetary union exercise any direct influences on the socio-economic structure to compensate for this loss of adjustment possibility? Fleming[6] has suggested that a certain disinflationary effect may result in members with a fast rate of price increase from an awareness among the principal decision-takers in government and industry of the greater dangers inherent in high rates of inflation within a monetary union. This conclusion, however, seems improbable. It greatly overestimates the ability of such decision-takers to control the fundamental socio-economic problems, even given the awareness that the escape hatch of devaluation has been closed.

Another possible compensating mechanism is the same institutional equalisation of wages that is thought to produce the immediate problems for previously low-wage national regions. Once wages have risen to the overall Community level, presumably the same institutional forces would tend to keep them in line. However, other variables summarised in the national propensity to inflate would continue to exert some pressure on the national-regional price-level. Thus, while the most serious impact may be in the early years of a monetary union while wages were catching up, the difficulties would also persist over a longer period.

The conclusion is that, in the face of markedly different socio-economic structures any attempt at economic integration must provide for adjustment, either through the exchange rate mechanism[7] or via an alternative means, the only likely alternative being intra-Community transfers among the national regions.

The Effects of Monetary Union on Sub-Regions

The effects on sub-regions may be divided into two kinds. First, there are effects which derive from a varying incidence on different sub-regions of the effects on national economies which have already been analysed above. Secondly, there are effects which relate to the specific circumstances of each sub-region. While some general analysis may apply to the former, only a detailed analysis of the industrial situation of each sub-region in the Community could clarify the effects under the latter heading. If monetary union means that uncompetitive national regions must deflate aggregate demand as an alternative to parity changes, the question arises as to whether deflation or devaluation are preferable on account of the way they distribute the costs of adjustment among the sub-regions. Devaluation lowers the price level relatively to foreigners for the whole country. In so far as sub-regions suffer from relatively high unemployment and/or low incomes on account of foreign competition with exported or import-competing production (as in the cases of Lancashire textiles or Scottish shipbuilding), a devaluation of the national currency may be specially beneficial to them, and all the more so since the costs of the deterioration in the terms of trade will be borne by the whole national population in higher prices of imported food, raw materials and components.

Greater differences exist with respect to the level of economic development among sub-regions in the Community than among national regions, and some of the less productive sub-regions might face major difficulties. Less competitive regions like Scotland or Sicily will be faced with competition not only from more competitive regions within the old nation states, for example, South East England and Piedmont, but from regions such as Baden-Wurttemberg whose competitiveness is even greater.

It could be argued that a region like Baden-Wurttemberg will compete with a region such as the West Midlands having a similar economic structure, both regions excelling in the production of light manufactures and modern, science-based products, rather than with the products of a region like Scotland, depending more on traditional heavy industries. But in a less prosperous region like Scotland there would be an increased danger to the light manufacturing sector, which plays a significant role in the regional economy. In particular the attempt to diversify the Scottish economy by an extension of this sector, for example by the industries being established in Scotland's New Towns, could be threatened.

Adjustment of Disequilibria with Factor Mobility

The assumption of factor immobility may now be relaxed. The extent to which disequilibria among both national regions and sub-regions will persist within a European monetary union will in practice be influenced by the degree and kinds of mobility of capital and labour. Thus national regions or sub-regions having a payment deficit and faced with the prospect of having to increase the level of unemployment, could solve the problem either by attracting outside capital or by promoting emigration of labour. In the absence of restrictions, and under classical assumptions, this inter-regional factor movement would take place naturally in response to differential factor earnings to re-establish an equilibrium situation.

But this classical economic thoery envisaging an optimal allocation in response to marginal differences in factor prices is quite inadequate to explain the likely developments inside a European economic and monetary union. In practice regional problems have been found to persist inside national economies over periods of many decades despite the tendency for these automatic adjustments to correct them. Factor movements may also have disequilibrating effects. And even equilibrating factor movements may have undesirable and unacceptable side-effects. We can analyse the possible development and effects of short-, medium- and long-term capital movements and of short-, medium- and long-term labour movements. However, the most interesting question, central to regional policy in the existing member states, is whether or not outflows of capital and labour in the adjustment of regional economies would lead to a cumulative decline. Thus the 'solution' implied in the formation of a monetary union in the absence of a satisfactory regional policy may be precisely what many would view as the essence of the regional problem. The examination of factor mobility indicates that it may not be a cure, but rather an acceptance that we must live with the disease. The case for a meaningful Community regional policy, far from being denied, is thus underlined.

Capital Mobility

The establishment of a monetary union of the single-currency type should eliminate inter-regional flows of exchange-speculative capital; this is indeed a major advantage of the establishment of such a union, an advantage not altogether shared by a union of the parallel currency or key currency types, which may still leave scope for short-term speculation.

In the medium term the effect of capital flows in a monetary union is less clear. Classical economic theory assumed that in a situation of inter-regional payments disequilibrium compensating flows of capital would take place in response to differential interest rates. Thus capital would flow from regions with a payments surplus but relatively low interest rates to regions of payments deficit with relatively high interest rates, tending to restore equilibrium. However, there is also a possibility that medium-term capital movements would be disequilibrating, depending on the relative changes between the incentive to invest and the incentive to save in the respective regions.

The regional imbalance is likely to be aggravated by the tendency for the surplus regions to be more concerned with their internal inflation rates than with their external balances, with the result that they frequently accentuate the payments problem by raising interest rates in order to reduce the rate of domestic inflation. The foreign capital attracted by this increase in interest rates adds to the money supply, thus bringing new difficulties in the control of domestic inflation. Measures to neutralise the inflow by controls in the surplus region would not prevent harmful outflow from the deficit region. The creation of a unified capital market is often considered both an objective of and a requirement for monetary union. If, however, the impact on national regions were disequilibrating, a unified capital market might be undesirable.

In the long term, following the creation of a unified capital market, interest rates are likely to be equalised. However, this process would be fairly gradual, and even if it were complete the possibility of capital flows being completely eliminated is slim, since in the long term capital flows are decided by the levels of actual and expected economic activity and profitability of industries located in a particular region, rather than by relative interest rates.[8]

Labour Mobility

Short-term inter-regional labour flows (defined as the daily or weekly movement of workers across the national-regional or sub-regional frontiers within the Community) will take place not only as a result of any regional differences in wages, but also because of the availability of employment in some regions, compared to the limited employment opportunities in others. They are likely to have a stabilising effect upon the regional economies, since the outflow of labour from the less productive regions will reduce the extent of unemployment in these regions, while the inflow into the more productive regions will ease inflationary pressures there. But really short-term labour flows are limited to short distances between contiguous members, that is largely to the Benelux area and the Franco-German and Franco-Italian frontier districts.

In the medium term, inter-regional labour flows (defined as the movement of individual workers across regional boundaries for long periods, but without their families) may continue to ease the problems of labour shortage and help to relieve inflation in the more productive regions. Further advantages derive from the temporary nature of the migrant work force. A cyclical downturn in the regional economy may be mitigated to some degree by a reduction of the migrant labour force, thus minimising the increase in the unemployment rate of the indigenous work force. As a result regional growth is likely to be more sustained and even. A second, less easily quantifiable, but probably important advantage to the labour-importing region is the economy in social provision such as housing which a temporary and alien work force may allow. However, these economic advantages may be offset by unacceptable social and political costs. The weakening of the indigenous trade unions which is implicit in the import of migrant labour and in the attempt to curb cost inflation in the absence of a coherent incomes policy may provoke political opposition and prove unacceptable.

Labour flows may have more serious effects in the less prosperous regions. Migration usually involves the elite of the regional working population, the young and the well-educated who already hold jobs. Their emigration tends to leave vacancies that cannot necessarily be filled by the regional unemployed; so unemployment may not be greatly reduced, while the absence of a skilled labour force discourages new investment. The only alternative for those wishing to invest in the region is to attempt to attract labour from outside by raising earnings in key posts towards the levels which prevail in more prosperous regions. This in turn may, by removing the 'natural' offset of lower wages, render the enterprise unviable. Indeed, unattractive regions may even have to raise earnings in some occupations above the levels prevailing elsewhere in order to attract key workers, thus increasing the locational disadvantages of the region. Emigration will also have a deflationary effect by reducing the total available regional income. Even if migration involves the hitherto unemployed section of the working population the subsequent reduction of regional income by the loss of income derived from unemployment benefits will, in the absence of an alternative method of injecting money into the regional economy, result in further deflation; though the regional income gains from remittances of emigrant workers, and this can be a significant advantage, since the cost of regional income maintenance is transferred to more prosperous regions.

If the migration becomes long-term (defined as the permanent movement of workers with their families, taking up normal residence and eventually citizenship, in the regions of immigration) the consequences could be unfavourable for both importing and exporting regions. In the prosperous, labour-importing region permanent immigration may add to inflationary pressure on account of the investment needs of immigrants. Stability is only likely if, as in Germany, propensities to save are high, both among the indigenous population and among the immigrants, and if the government is able to keep its expenditure down.

B. Community Regional Policy

Adam Ridley

Following the analysis of the kind Geoffrey Denton has undertaken of the possible regional implications of the EMU, one may begin by some basic premises outlining the sort of developments in the regional problem which one anticipates in the enlarged community.

As time passes, the agricultural aspect of the regional problem will dwindle to insignificance, but the industrial will not. Whether or not there is an EMU, accelerating technical progress and growing industrial concentration will speed up the process of structural change and accentuate tendencies to cumulative vicious and virtuous circles in the process of regional development in the Nine. The current energy crisis will probably reinforce them. Progress towards EMU in areas other than regional policy is likely to reinforce and unlikely to offset these tendencies.

Progress to EMU will favour mobility of capital more than mobility of labour, at least for a considerable time if not indefinitely. This may also be expected to aggravate regional imbalances.

The adverse influence of differential rates of inflation will come into play if exchange rates are locked; if wage bargaining is conducted in terms of Europas/Dollars or other international units of currency; or if international parity of real earnings is effectively pursued by employees in most or all of the Nine.

Given such premises one concludes that the need for regional policies in the enlarged Community is likely to increase rather than decline for some considerable time to come.

Objectives

It is very common to find that the objectives of any actual or hypothetical regional policies are very inadequately specified. We must therefore begin by establishing and characterising the chief alternatives which are possible.

The negative objectives of regional policy can be most simply regarded as aspects of the goal of integrated markets and fair competition which is shared both by individual countries and by the Community. These are simply to ensure that whatever is done to alleviate regional problems should not distort competition, or lead to the misallocation of resources in any static sense.

Among positive objectives, the elimination of divergences between actual or expected income distribution and some desired distribution is important. In a very egalitarian world the aim would naturally be thought of in rather static terms as largely or totally eliminating disparities in regional income per head. In circumstances more like those currently prevailing, the aim might be something vaguer and less comprehensive, for example, to prevent a widening of unevenness (variance) in the distribution of average regional GDP or household income per capita, and to raise the per capita income levels in the poorest areas. This objective can be met directly either by redistributive policy instruments such as transfer payments, or in a less efficient and more indirect way by intervention in the location of production and investment.

A more traditional set of policy aims is to act to correct one or more of the three classic symptons of labour market disequilibrium by: the elimination of differentials in unemployment rates; the reduction of net emigration; and by equalisation of activity rates and job opportunities. Each of these three aims is a partial reflection of the degree of health (or equilibrium) of the labour market. Taken together they characterise it fully. The presence of any one of these symptoms means that the national labour market is not as fair and efficient as it ought ideally to be.

Finally one must consider briefly two rather more metaphysical aims that are very closely related if not in some cases identical. The phrase 'balanced regional economy' and others like it characterise a situation in which a region suffers from no defect (over-dependence on a narrow range of employers, industries, etc.) so serious that it will be prevented from progressing satisfactorily under its own steam, that is from achieving self-sustaining growth. Put slightly differently, the thought is that one is concerned with situations, not merely where things are wrong (above average emigration or unemployment), but where the region cannot put them right itself without outside assistance except, possibly, by efforts which would place an unjustly heavy burden on the region.

Conditions for a Community Regional Policy

Some of the most interesting and important aspects of a Community Regional Policy (CRP) arise not in choosing and defining its objectives, difficult though this is, but in considering what further conditions should be met by a CRP. The issues at stake are of considerable current and practical importance, but they are not all economic.

Efficiency

It is axiomatic that we should want any policy, including a CRP, to be efficient. What does this imply in narrow *economic* terms? It is unfortunately very difficult to answer this question, as there has been woefully little theoretical and almost no empirical work on the resource costs and benefits of regional policies or instruments. In the absence of such work there are a number of maxims or principles which are relevant. There seems to be a strong case for saying that to be effective a regional policy must be both selective and positive. It must set quite specific goals: to develop area A rather than B, to encourage activity C or firm D. The provision of macro-incentives alone cannot be as effective. It involves an essentially passive response to requests for assistance rather than a coherent attempt to alter the evolution of a region. In so doing it cannot have regard to the special problems of differing localities, nor can it stimulate and exploit local knowledge and enthusiasm.

Operating subsidies to industry are probably less efficient in stimulating expansion and relocation than 'one-off' grants toward investment, training or costs of movement. They are often little more than unplanned and indiscriminate income transfers. Theoretical similarity between most forms of regionally differentiated subsidy enables one to reduce their values to a uniform measure such as reduction in costs of production or increase in expected rate of return. However this approach ignores the important practical question of the conditions and circumstances under which assistance is offered. Just as the discriminating monopolist makes more profits by partitioning his market and extracting the maximum price for his product from each buyer, selective policies aimed only at those who are potentially responsive are likely to have smaller cost and larger benefits than general passive macro ones.

There is also an *administrative* aspect to efficiency. Should the administration (and the devising and financing) of regional policies be centralised or decentralised? Those who share the writer's view that a measure of decentralisation is necessary[9] even inside a country of the size of Italy, France or the United Kingdom will probably agree that some degree of administrative decentralisation is all the more necessary in the administration of the regional policy of a much larger Community.

There are, finally, *political* considerations as well. Regional policy is highly political and non-economic considerations play a large role in decisions both at the very local level and at the centre. A CRP must not increase the likelihood of politically attractive but economically lunatic location decisions, such as putting new steel plants in every depressed area in the Community. Nor, if decentralised, should a CRP be allowed to become the fief of parochial and unrealistically competitive local politicians, bureaucrats or entrepreneurs. Finally, one should perhaps add that one must anticipate some machinery for democratic control for a CRP. Such machinery is unfortunately likely to be particularly difficult to construct, because it raises awkward political and constitutional problems for several members of the Community.

Acceptability

Conditions for efficiency such as those outlined above are something which enlightened observers might like to see met. The ones we consider next are those which individual countries and the Commission are likely to *demand* to be fulfilled if they are to consent to movement toward a genuine and significant CRP.

There are, first, tensions between the desire for a degree of national or local autonomy and a degree of central control in devising and implementing Community and national policies. National governments are likely to want to keep a considerable measure of independence for a long time to come for purely political reasons, quite apart from any considerations of efficiency, although there may of course be an indirect connection between the two motives. This would lead them to favour a CRP which simply reimburses them for what they would undertake anyway. On the other hand most governments, and the Commission itself, will want to control and put constraints on what other member governments are doing with their regional policies and on what is done in other countries under the CRP. In particular, the higher the level of expenditure under a CRP, the greater will be the interest of those making the larger net financial contributions in ensuring that the money is spent in ways which seem to be sensible; and at the same time the smaller will be the scope for purely national activity. Policy would therefore have to become genuinely *communautaire*. It may be that some compromise approach can be found which, with sensible objectives, offers both sufficient control to permit a broad and well-financed CRP and a generous degree of autonomy. However, until now there has been little progress on this front. In its absence one can only speculate on how far a CRP will develop. For our purposes the important question is whether it can develop into the sort of policy required for EMU?

Second, member states will seek a CRP having financial consequences which are broadly predictable for some time ahead. Possible net losers of resources will clearly want to know what sort of demands will be made of them. Possible gainers will want to know whether the net returns will be large enough to merit the effort. The larger the scale of planned expenditure under the CRP, the greater the interest in knowing what the CRP will involve. The desire to know may not be *communautaire,* but it is easy to understand in the early stages of progress to economic union.

Third, there is the very important problem of accommodating the financial aspects of a CRP in the Community budget. While the Report of the Study Group[10] suggests that substantial expenditures can be accommodated under certain circumstances, one must recognise that budget constraints may nonetheless be serious.

There is a Commission doctrine of 'complementarity' or 'additionality', whereby its own expenditure programmes should not replace the related national policies in part or whole, but should supplement them. There are, of course, certain possibilities of actions for genuine Community objectives, such as Community-wide transport schemes or the well-known transfrontier problems. But with these limited exceptions it is difficult to conceive of types of intervention which national governments do not and should not want to undertake themselves. A CRP which claimed too much for itself would soon run into difficulties, both analytical and practical. On the face of it a CRP which permitted the total resources devoted to regional development to be increased would be the more acceptable proposition. But even on this interpretation care would have to be taken. There are genuine risks that too many marginal and unviable projects or programmes might be aided. These risks must be minimised, even if some of those who express concern about them do so with specious arguments and for cynical motives.

Machinery

The various ways in which a CRP might operate have been rather neglected, even in informed discussion. We must therefore discuss possible types of machinery, considering how well they meet the possible objectives of a regional policy.

Negative controls to protect competition

As is well know, the Competition Directorate-General of the Commission has already gone some way in developing procedures to reduce distortions and waste of resources by defining central and peripheral areas, setting ceilings on aids in central areas, and by instituting provisions for transparency and for the use of certain approved policy instruments. This initiative can be welcomed, at least in broad terms, and has gone some way to increase the possibility of running an efficient and positive regional policy. It can profitably be taken some way further, subject to certain changes of emphasis. There are, however, risks that it might in time attempt to impose arbitrary uniformity and restrictions where these are an obstacle to the genuine local needs of a region, an affront to the legitimate interests of local or national politicians and an unnecessary complication in the operation of a CRP.

Co-ordination of present policies

There is in principle also a case for trying to ensure coherence between objectives, instruments and decisions in the policies of national governments. In practical terms this might involve a fairly motley range of actions such as: reconciling policies pursued, or developments occurring, on either side of a border between member countries where the policies pursued are inconsistent or the developments conflicting; preventing national authorities from actions such as simultaneously bailing out all declining shipbuilding industries in the Community in the name of regional development; rationalising multifarious and self-defeating attempts to attract foreign investors. It is probable that there would be a number of unspectacular fields in which such co-ordination would be efficient or worthwhile. Unfortunately the Commission has not succeeded in past attempts to co-ordinate national policies, perhaps because it has concentrated more on the general rather than the particular. Some limited degree of co-ordination would almost certainly be acceptable before long, and it would certainly pay dividends.

Financing Projects

Probably, but not necessarily, through the agency of a Regional Development Fund (RDF), a CRP could in principle finance a wide range of individual projects in member states. It could lend or grant money directly to infrastructure projects, retraining and conversion schemes and to enterprises in the private and public sectors. The relevant authorities would forward dossiers of applications for assistance to the RDF by whom each case would be vetted. This procedure is followed already by the EIB, the FEOGA Structural Fund, and by many other bodies such as the World Bank. It can be followed whether the RDF is financing all or part of a project, with or without the participation of national authorities.

The projects approach offers useful opportunities for exercising negative controls and positive co-ordination, though neither objective could be achieved unless special procedures were built into the vetting process. It is easy to see it being used to promote the positive objectives of labour market equilibrium or self-sustaining growth.

One must however have doubts whether the projects approach would be either efficient or acceptable if the RDF Budget approached the sort of size many people would like to see. Even to process project applications concerned with infrastructure and training, quite a substantial staff would be needed. Processing much more numerous applications for grant or loan assistance by individual firms would be considerably more laborious and inefficient.[11] One may doubt whether the work could or should be done by an RDF in Brussels if the RDF is to deal expeditiously with the cases of individual firms. And a whole further dimension of difficulties would arise if one wanted to have the RDF play an active and positive role in seeking out projects to assist, rather than having it react passively to proposals from elsewhere.

Whatever the force of this argument, it seems highly improbable that the Commission would want to set up a large bureaucratic RDF, or that member countries would find such a proposal acceptable. If one wanted the RDF to get involved in large-scale project vetting or project initiation, it would be better to do so in concert with local bodies such as the Irish Development Authority, the Cassa or the German Lander; or it might choose to run some agencies of its own in individual regions. This might well be more efficient, and one might encounter fewer difficulties in obtaining the consent of member countries, though they would still be certain to raise objections.

One should note that with a pure projects approach it may not always be easy to guarantee or predict what the net receipts or contributions of a state will be. The financial outcome will in principle be a function of the efficiency of each country relative to the others in putting forward projects acceptable to the REF, and this may well be an indeterminate and unpredictable process, unless the RDF operates with some sort of system of national quotas. If they do the latter, other problems would arise; for example, if the demands for assistance (which would have to be at standard rates) exceeded the funds available. But the projects approach is clearly of little use if the major object of the RDF is to redistribute income.

Supporting approved national policy instruments

A simple way in which a CRP might operate, particularly at the beginning, would be for the Commission to subsidise the policy instruments of member governments. The essence of such an approach might be —

(1) the Commission would agree areas in which it would defray part of the cost of national policies and, at least in rough terms, the degree of need of each region;

(2) governments would have to use only a selection of policy instruments approved under rules of the CRP;

(3) the Commission or RDF would reimburse standard proportions of expenditure incurred in approved areas through approved policies;

(4) the support might be made conditional on some degree of co-ordination of policies at Community level.

This approach might offer *en passant* a way of achieving the negative objectives of co-ordination. It would be of unpredictable use as a tool for income redistribution; much would depend on what form national policies take, for example whether they included regionally-differentiated transfer payments of various kinds. Its effectiveness in achieving the positive objectives would depend on how good national policies are. If the mainly macro weapons which now predominate are not sufficient to cure serious regional problems, as was argued above, then this sort of CRP would not be adequate on its own. The approach would be acceptable without doubt to some members of the Community, but would perhaps not be welcomed widely as a major part of a CRP in the long run, since it would not offer much scope for developing naturally into a Community policy with real content.

Once the course and scale of national expenditure is determined, one would only require knowledge of the defined areas and degree of assistance to calculate a future distribution of receipts from such a policy. There is a real risk, however, that it might have the unattractive result of tempting member countries to produce dishonestly inflated classifications of regional policy expenditure.

There are many other ways in which the expenditure could be allocated. The amount of money to be allocated to a country could be calculated on the basis of need without direct reference to the scale of national expenditure. The predictability of the outcome would then depend on the criteria for need selected, the degree to which they are stable and the extent to which they are open to modification by direct political pressure. Obvious criteria are such indicators as income levels or job requirements. Other relevant ones can also be derived from inter-regional comparisons of infrastructure.[12] However, a considerable amount of new data and analysis is needed before one can get a meaningful measure of need which is uncontroversial. The working out of criteria for need is obviously something with highly political implications. What has up till now been a fairly arcane corner of applied regional economics may have to be exposed to public scrutiny before long, and the results will reflect little credit on the competence of the economists or the honesty of the politicians. Any attempts to develop criteria of need should be related to the possible objectives of policy. If one is primarily concerned with labour-market equilibrium, the most interesting criteria will be built up from a picture of emigration, future redundancies, and differentials in unemployment and activity rates. If one is concerned with income levels, earned or otherwise, then regional GDP *per capita* will be of interest. An objective of self-sustaining growth might require a much more complicated set of diagnostic criteria; the current state of the regional balance of payments would not be sufficient.

Supporting programmes

The terms 'plan' and 'programme' are vague, but quite often used in the context of a CRP, no doubt in a number of different senses. One might imagine a programme-based CRP which worked roughly as follows. The Commission would agree areas to be assisted, policy instruments, and enforce transparency conditions and so on. Each member state would submit periodically a regional development plan or programme for each area eligible for assistance from the RDF. The plan would specify the objectives to be pursued in each case and the means to those ends. It would cover not merely the requirements of job creation but wider issues such as housing, transport, education and training, and would try to draw together a range of coherent actions which would together assist the region's development. The Commission would examine the programme; if it approved the proposals it would support the programme as an entity rather than specific projects, expenditure classes or instruments involved in it. The RDF would advance money to the national government or regional body responsible on a basis to be specified, for example, on a need criterion such as GDP per head. The expenditure would be monitored and reviewed to some extent by RDF personnel stationed in the region, who might also have some part to play in the execution of the programme.

The sort of area for which a programme would be produced might be a *formally* constituted region such as Sardinia, a geographically and economically coherent area like South Wales or, more exceptionally, a smaller area facing particularly acute problems. There would sometimes be difficulties in finding an administrative or political authority which corresponded to the boundaries which might be appropriate.

Apart from a general concern with co-ordination and coherence, which might justify the RDF in focusing *ad hoc* in some detail and if need by wielding a veto on a number of individual projects despite its general programme approval, the national and local authorities would be free to implement the programme once it was approved. This would help to meet an important necessary condition for efficiency, that of a substantial measure of decentralisation. The monitoring and reviewing process and the need to roll forward and resubmit programmes would give the RDF regular opportunities to check on the cost-effectiveness of the administration of the system.

When dealing with such a vague blue-print it is very difficult to predict how acceptable it would be. It would give each country through the medium of the Commission and the RDF quite a powerful say in the shaping of a CRP and in the actions of national and local authorities. At the same time it would leave a great deal of independence in the hands of those responsible for executing policy. If it were accepted, it would have to be developed largely from scratch, though there are instructive analogies from which a useful start could be made, for example, in the procedures followed by the World Bank.

Systems of Community Transfer Payments

Redistributional objectives could be met simply in a number of ways by introducing a Community element into such instruments as social security or unemployment contributions and payments. For example, the harmonisation of benefits to standard levels throughout the Community could redistribute income between *countries,* assuming contributions were *not* harmonised; the institution of higher levels of benefit or lower levels of contribution in problem areas inside a member country could be made to achieve a similar effect, if the programme were subsidised by the Community. In this case no harmonisation of social security systems would be needed.

Physical Controls and Negative Inducements

British experience with Industrial Development Certificates (IDCs) suggests strongly that physical controls and negative inducements can play a useful role in achieving positive objectives. There is no necessity for them to play a part in a CRP in the medium to long term. But they might be valuable at the Community level, for example if centripetal forces towards 'Lotharingia' were to get out of hand in the longer term.

Concluding observations

As at the time of writing the Community has not yet reached any decision about the creation of a Regional Development Fund or the broad lines of its regional policy, there may be some value in outlining some of the practical considerations and the elementary analysis of possible objectives which will have to be dealt with before concrete progress can be made. But the discussion should not be closed without posing what may be considered to be a fundamental question about the role of a Community regional policy. It is widely argued in the United Kingdom and elsewhere that some members of the Community, of which the United Kingdom might be one, could be vulnerable to declining competitiveness if and when parities are locked in EMU. The relevant analysis has been set out in the first part of this chapter. The conventional remedy to that hypothetical problem is considered to be a Community regional policy. But can a CRP be expected to do what is required of it?

The optimist might argue that a CRP could tackle such a situation by subsidising social security and by massive assistance to correct the uncompetitive industrial structure of the country in question, possibly augmented by subsidies such as the Regional Employment Premium if these are thought useful. This combination of instruments would maintain incomes in the short-term until the longer-term changes in industrial structure which are required could be effected.

A pessimist might argue that a locking of parities under circumstances roughly like those of today could create a swift and fairly dramatic decline in competitiveness, not so much because of a fundamental and slow-changing weakness in technology but merely because of changes in the movement of relative wage costs. Such a deterioration would require very large and quickly growing transfers to sustain incomes and demand. And structural policies to alter competitiveness by raising productivity would be very slow to act, unreliable at best, and their benefits could be quickly negated by a renewed burst of wage inflation. The pessimist could argue in general terms that structural, supply-side policies are not a suitable way of dealing with demand-side problems of uncompetitive costs.

If the pessimist is right, then it will only be prudent to lock parities when there has been genuine, near total and irreversible convergence of productivity and earnings trends throughout the Community. The main role of a CRP would then be restricted to assisting development in sub-regions, just as national regional policy is today, and while some inter-state transfers would inevitably emerge, as argued on pp. 69-70, CRP would not be called on, untried, to do duty as a novel system of international aid. Only in such propitious circumstances can a CRP be politically acceptable.

But we must not forget that even with floating exchange rates one would suffer from the vices of locked parities without their virtues if wage negotiations in the lower productivity countries of the Community were based on the aim of real wage parity or were indexed to the unit of account. The uncompetitive countries might then be very glad of a CRP, whatever its deficiencies.

References

1. R.A. Mundell, 'A Theory of Optimum Currency Areas', *American Economic Review,* Vol. 51, September 1961.
2. *Report on Regional Problems in the Enlarged European Community,* Com (73) 550 final. Brussels, 3 May 1973.
3. See below, pp. 86-7 for a discussion of programme aid.
4. See, for example, G R. Denton and S. O'Cleireacain, *Subsidy Issues in International Commerce,* Trade Policy Research Centre, London, November 1972.
5. See G. Magnifico, 'European Monetary Integration for Balanced Growth: a new approach,' *Princeton Essays in International Commerce,* No. 58, August 1972; and the same author's *European Monetary Unification,* Macmillan, London, 1973.
6. J.M. Fleming, 'On Exchange Rate Unification', *Economic Journal,* September 1971.
7. This conclusion was reached by Meade and Balassa, writing in the late 1950s and early 1960s. Meade was referring to the EEC customs union, a more limited experiment in integration than the monetary union with which Balassa was concerned. Balassa in particular, having examined the case against flexible exchange rates, felt that just such flexibility was called for during a transitional period prior to the internal adjustment of the regional economies.
8. For a fuller account of capital market problems in an EMU, see Chapter 3 above.
9. And has proved beneficial for industrial development both in Ulster and in Germany.
10. *Economic Union in the EEC,* Croom Helm for the Federal Trust, 1974. See also Chapter 7 below.
11. It is worth remembering that a common criticism of the system of investment grants introduced in the United Kingdom in the late 1960s was that it was slow, remote and inefficient. The offices responsible for processing the applications were also considered too far away in London.
12. See the French Fifth Plan, 1966-70, for examples.

6 FISCAL ISSUES

Alan Prest

This chapter will be concerned initially with matters of tax harmonisation, specifically with respect to Value-Added Tax (VAT) and Corporation Tax. It might be asked immediately why discussion of tax harmonisation should be confined to the above two taxes. The answer is quite simply that it is much more of a live issue in these two cases than with, say, personal income tax or taxes on capital; and great as the difficulties of harmonisation may be with VAT and Corporation Tax, they would seem to be even more in practice with excise duties, and so less capable of resolution.

A. VAT Harmonisation

We shall start by setting out the objectives of harmonisation; say something about present VAT structures in member countries; then discuss the attributes of the different forms which VAT can in principle take; and finally appraise the changes which are needed.

Objectives of Harmonisation

As is well known, harmonisation is a multi-headed concept; it can be made to mean almost anything, if enough ingenuity is exercised. In the context of VAT, it would seem important to distinguish three different objectives. First, taxes in member countries need to be such as not to interfere with trade flows between them, in the sense of altering the relative advantages of different locations of production. There is not much point, it is argued, in making great efforts to abolish tariff barriers, differential subsidies and the like if VAT arrangements are such as to impede trade flows. This proposition applies to international trading relationships generally but even more so in a free trade area. Second, there is the objective of abolishing fiscal frontiers. This becomes possible when a customs union, with a common external tariff, is formed, as in that case imports into the union are subject to the same rate of import duty irrespective of the point of entry. So it is no longer necessary to have check-points on intra-Community frontiers to ensure the charging of the rate of import duty appropriate to any one member.

If in addition VAT can be collected on domestically-produced goods at the point of origin (and on imported ones at the point of entry) then all goods can travel without let or hindrance between member countries.

Both these aims; abolition of taxes impeding flows of goods between countries and abolition of taxes and customs procedures at frontiers, were very much in mind during the development of the Community in the 1960s. But more recently, with the advent of the economic and monetary union proposals, a third objective for VAT has become important: the need to finance the Community budget and the decision to raise part of this finance through VAT. This has two implications, the first being the need for a sufficiently common base on which the Community tax can be levied, and the second the need to fit Community and member country VAT levies together in such a way as not to impede individual countries' stabilisation, income distribution or regional policies.

It seems best to define harmonisation of VAT in terms of these three aims of abolishing impediments to goods flows, abolishing fiscal frontiers and financing the Community without undue member-country side-effects. We shall see later whether or not fulfilment of these aims entails standardisation of coverage, rates, etc. For the time being, we keep open the likelihood that harmonisation implies something less than complete standardisation.

Current VAT Structures[1]

Since 1973, all nine member countries have levied VAT and there are many similarities of tax structure. The consumption variant of the tax (purchases of capital goods are a deductible input just like any other input on current account) has been chosen in preference to the income variant (depreciation, but not capital expenditure is deductible). In all cases the tax is levied on a destination rather than an origin basis, that is, exports are free of tax but imports are taxable. And the indirect method of computing tax liabilities (first calculate tax due on turnover but then deduct that paid on inputs to reach the net sum payable) is preferred to direct computation of valued added in all but a few special cases. This procedure is adopted so as to secure as much self-policing of tax collection as possible, in the sense that it will always be to the advantage of any one firm to ensure that VAT has been paid by its suppliers of materials or services.

Nevertheless, wide differences between VAT structures remain. The coverage differs enormously from country to country, both with respect to the exclusion of particular goods and services and of particular types of enterprise (at retail level; or below a certain size of turnover). The ways in which exclusions are made also differ: in some cases all services are within the scope of the tax apart from specified exceptions, whereas

in others only a list of taxable services is given. Rate structures also
differ very considerably as the following table shows:

VAT Effective Rates Per Cent 1973

France	7	17.6	20.0	33.3
W.Germany	5.5	-	11	-
Netherlands	4	-	16	-
Belgium	6	14	18	25
Luxembourg	5	-	10	-
Ireland	5.26	11.11	16.37	30.26
Denmark	-	-	15	-
U.K.	-	-	10	-
Italy	3	6	12	18

Note: An *effective* rate of VAT is defined as the rate on price
excluding tax, as compared to a *nominal* rate on price
including tax. Writing *te* for effective rate and *tn* for
nominal rate, we have

$$te = \frac{tn}{1 - tn} \quad \text{and} \quad tn = \frac{te}{1 + te}$$ Hence a 20%
nominal rate corresponds to a 25% effective rate.

Several features of this table are worth noting. One is that the level
of rates differs between 3 per cent and 33.3 per cent; a second is that
the number of rates differs between one and four. Furthermore, the
concept of a 'zero rate' is especially important in the UK; in effect this
means that although an item is within the scope of the tax no tax is
payable so that, effectively, there are two rates in the UK: 0 per cent
and 10 per cent. Finally, it should be stressed that the rates shown in
the table are those appearing in the statute book; they are not
necessarily fully observed in practice and there is in fact good reason to
believe that the degree of observance varies from country to country.

Theoretical aspects[2]
These are partly a matter of efficiency and partly of equity.
    If we first consider a *destination* type of tax it can in principle be
general (one rate of tax applied to all goods and services consumed by
persons) or selective (differential tax rates). With a *destination-general*
tax in Country A, there is clearly no differentiation between home-
produced and imported items in that country. The *modus operandi*
depends on whether product prices are assumed to rise or factor prices
to fall, on whether there is any flexibility of exchange rates and on the
particular assumptions about the correspondence of spending by

government out of the tax proceeds with the personal spending which would have taken place in the absence of the tax.

But the general proposition of no differentiation holds.

Similarly, if we have a *destination-selective* tax (assuming that the basis of selection is not according to whether a commodity is imported or home-produced). Although such a tax will affect relative consumption of goods and services and although the total volume of trade between countries may also be affected, there is no change in relative advantages of producing in one place rather than another.

Turning to an *origin-general* tax in A, it is instructive to work through the results, assuming product prices to rise. A's exports will now be less competitive than before and, on the other hand, it will be a bigger magnet for imports. So its exchange rate tends to fall and by this means exports remain competitive abroad and prices of imports rise in terms of domestic currency. Once again we have the same result; nothing has happened to change relative advantages of production in different locations. If the exchange rate is fixed, equilibrium could be restored by an export rebate and a compensating import duty. And if factor prices fall instead of product prices rising, we still have the same end-result as before.

With an *origin-selective* tax the position is very different. If an exporting country imposes such a tax on a particular product, this has effects exactly parallel to those of a tariff imposed by an importing country. Domestic products tend to be substituted for imports and so we do now have both a reduction in the volume of trade and a change in the location of production. This is not to say that one particular country may not benefit, but simply that there is a loss from a world viewpoint.

So the overall result from an efficiency viewpoint is that comparative costs are unaffected by a destination tax, whatever its form, nor does it matter from this standpoint if an origin-general tax is imposed; it is only an origin-selective tax which causes trouble.

Concerning equity, the central question is whether foreign consumers should pay part of the tax. There is no clear-cut guide here but if the view is taken that foreigners should not be taxed, this points to the destination rather than the origin basis.

Necessary Changes

What changes are necessary in the present structure of VAT in member countries, if the various objectives of policy are to be achieved?

Taking impediments to trade first, we can see that the destination basis, whether general or selective, is perfectly satisfactory (unless imports are the basis of any selectivity); comparative costs are unaffected and so there is no cause for concern here. And if product prices are assumed to rise, rather than factor prices fall, there is no necessity to postulate flexible exchange rates. So on this score the current pattern of destination-selective taxes is acceptable.

The second objective was the abolition of fiscal frontiers. This clearly requires an origin basis of tax, at least for intra-EEC trade (a 'restricted origin' basis); otherwise VAT would still have to be collected at intra-Community frontiers. But if there has to be a move to an origin basis for this reason, the implications are far-reaching. As we have seen, an origin-selective tax would impede trade between countries. In other words, the only form of tax which would satisfy both the trade and the fiscal frontier objectives is an origin-general tax. Even though the rate of tax[3] need not be the same for each country (assuming some flexibility of exchange rates), the changes required would be very large all the same compared to the variegated picture shown earlier. One might, incidentally, query whether the administrative saving from customs abolition on intra-EEC trade would be so enormous; no doubt there are a number of border points inside the Community which are concerned with this type of trade only, but this would hardly be true of the UK and Ireland, for instance. And customs inspection may well be needed for checks on standards, illicit traffic and the like. This is not to ignore the symbolic aspects of customs abolition but simply to place it in its proper position.

The third objective is an appropriate form of VAT in the context of EMU. The first point is that it is not necessary to have identical VAT coverage in each member country to raise, say, a 1 per cent Community levy. As long as value added tax in a country can be *estimated* on a comparable basis from National Accounts data this will suffice as a base for such a contribution. After all, it is not a matter of the Community imposing its own tax collection mechanism in each country; the contribution must be collected and transmitted by member governments. So there is no argument on these grounds for origin rather than destination, or identical rather than variegated, coverage.

A second issue is whether the levying of a Community VAT will impair demand management powers in a member country. This does not seem to be a great danger. Member government VAT proceeds will fall automatically in a recession and can be cut further by reducing their tax rates, if necessary. Even if there is no means of cutting the Community rate, payments from a member country would still fall in a recession. So the net sacrifice in demand management powers would not seem to be enormous (quite apart from the whole question of whether governments exercise such powers at all wisely).

A third matter is regional imbalance. Assuming, for simplicity, that a whole country (and not just a part of it) suffers from structural imbalance, how would it fare under the two-part VAT system we are contemplating? As before, VAT collections by the member country and the Community will fall automatically, the greater the structural imbalance. One other point is also worth noticing. If the tax were on a restricted origin basis, any cut in rates would be analogous to a wage subsidy as far as intra-Community trade is concerned. This would not be so if the destination basis were in being. So this might be thought to be an advantage of the origin basis. A similar argument would apply in the demand management context; but less strongly than with regional imbalance in so far as we then have surplus labour but not surplus capital equipment; and therefore measures encouraging labour-intensive practices are highly apposite.

Conclusion

There would seem to be no great difficulty in applying the piggyback principle, with a Community VAT superimposed on a member country VAT. Whether the way forward set out in the *Sixth Directive*[4] is appropriate or not, depends on one's views about the importance of abolishing fiscal frontiers and the case, if any, for a form of VAT which can serve as a substitute for a wage subsidy. It is far from clear that those who favour one of these objectives necessarily favour the other. A destination-selective basis is perfectly acceptable in the context of removing impediments to trade flows and making contributions to the Community. In so far as moves towards greater uniformity do take place, then the Benelux agreement reported towards the end of 1973 (move closer together, but allow rate differences up to specified amounts) is the obvious model.

B. Corporation Tax Harmonisation

We shall look successively at the objectives of tax harmonisation with special reference to corporation tax, the characteristics of alternative corporation tax systems and the future policy implications.

Objectives

The objectives of corporation tax harmonisation differ from those found with VAT. In the first place, we are concerned more with removal of impediments to factor flows than goods flows. The main objective must be to ensure that differing corporation tax arrangements, whether in defining the tax base or in subjecting a given base to tax, do not interfere with the flow of capital between member countries. This implies that double taxation arrangements must be such as to give full credit for corporation taxes paid in other countries, as distinct from mere deductibility. While the latter is consonant with equity from a national viewpoint (home tax paid on a given total of income received in a country should be the same, irrespective of whether it is entirely domestic source income or foreign source income net of foreign taxes) the crediting arrangement ties in better with the concept of international equity (total tax paid, foreign plus domestic, should be the same for the same pre-tax total of income whatever the source). And it is reasonable to assume that an international equity concept is more appropriate in this context.

At the same time we must not close our eyes to the possible effects of corporation taxes on goods flows. A corporation tax which is passed forward has effects very similar to those of an origin-selective VAT. So what was said earlier about this brand of VAT would apply in the context of forward shifting of corporation taxes.

An entirely different objective is the possible ultimate use of corporation tax as a source of Community finance. There are some arguments in favour of such a development. It can be maintained that the central government has the main right to corporation tax revenue under most Federal constitutions and that one might under some circumstances prefer to have a source of Community finance which is related to profits rather than wages.[5] It is also frequently argued that it is appropriate for corporations to pay tax to the Community as they benefit from Community developments. But this contention is by no means a strong one; others benefit as well as corporations; measurement of benefits to corporations is by no means easy; and it is far from clear that any such benefits would be proportional to profits. If it were agreed eventually that corporation profits should be a source of Community finance, there would be two very different ways of achieving this end: one would be the replacement of the existing member country taxes by a common tax imposed at Community level whereas with the other one would retain member-country taxes but strive for sufficient uniformity to ensure that the Community levy could be imposed equitably. Such developments would raise many questions about the integration of corporation tax with member-country personal income taxes, the adequacy of their powers for stabilisation by fiscal means and so on. However, it would not seem that we need lose too much sleep on such issues, as the prospect of Community finance via corporation tax is not an immediate one.

Alternative Arrangements

We consider the rival claims of different corporation tax arrangements, first from a domestic and secondly from an international standpoint.

The main contrast on the domestic front is between a system where corporation tax is levied independently of personal income tax and one where there is some element of integration between the two taxes. The main methods of integration are the split rate or dividend-paid credit system (whereby undistributed profits are taxed more heavily than distributed but dividends are fully taxed under personal income tax) and the imputation or dividend-received credit system (whereby all corporate profits are taxed at the same rate whether distributed or undistributed but special credits are given to shareholders against personal income tax). In comparing the separate systems (as practised in Holland) with an integrated system (as in France or Germany) the two main issues are those of equity and the saving total.[6] From an equity viewpoint, it is hard to defend the separate system which encourages dividend retentions and, as a result, absolves rich shareholders from paying tax at the appropriate marginal rate on the dividends they would have otherwise received. On savings, the arguments are less clear-cut: there are firstly considerations about how much the saving total may be affected (more company but less personal saving with the separate system) and secondly about the 'quality' of saving (whether it is more likely to be ill-spent, the greater the proportion in the form of retained profits). In the comparison between the different forms of integration, there is very little to be said in the domestic context; broadly speaking, they can be arranged to give identical results except that the ratio of corporation to personal income tax is likely to differ. This may in turn be important if corporation taxes are deemed to be shifted forward; in such a case, the imputation variety would result in a larger fraction of any given tax burden being borne by consumers, relatively to the split rate system.

In the international setting, it will be convenient to assume first that the same type of corporation tax prevails in every member country. We shall come later to the situation where different types exist side by side.

If we look at direct investment first, it can very quickly be seen that the imputation system[7] raises a problem not found with the separate system. This can best be demonstrated by a simple example. Suppose France and Britain each have a corporation tax of 40 per cent, and that the separate system prevails in each country. Then the shareholders of a British company investing in France will, assuming the usual double taxation arrangements, be treated in exactly the same way for tax purposes as if the investment were in the UK; and the same will hold for French shareholders, *mutatis mutandis*. But now assume an imputation system; say, for simplicity, each country has the same system as that operating in Britain from April 1973, i.e. 50 per cent corporation tax and a gross-up and credit factor of 3/7. As a consequence, the shareholders of a British company investing in France would not be as well-treated as if the investment were in Britain[8] and the same would hold for French shareholders in a company investing in Britain. It must therefore follow that in these circumstances an imputation system would introduce a bias against foreign investment not found with the separate system. The words 'in these circumstances' are important: discrimination will not arise, for instance, if there are sufficient liabilities to corporation tax at home to absorb Advance Corporation Tax; and the element of discrimination will be less, the smaller the payout ratio. But when all this is allowed for, there is still likely to be some discrimination against outward investment at least in the absence of special countervailing measures. If so, we are then faced with the situation that whatever one does is wrong; an imputation (or split rate) system will tend to produce a better allocation of funds *within* a country but a worse allocation *between* countries relatively to a separate system.[9]

The same drawback does not arise with portfolio investment. If a Briton invests in France and a credit is available to him as it would be to a French shareholder in that firm or to a British shareholder in a British firm, then there is no impediment to capital flows, over and above the nuisance of collecting tax credits from abroad. Such a system of credits depends on the negotiation of appropriate double taxation agreements but in practice this does not seem to occasion undue difficulty.

Now consider what happens if the corporation tax system of one member country differs from that of another. If the UK is on a split rate system and Holland on a separate system there is a strong temptation for Dutch subsidiaries operating in the UK to maximise dividends to parent companies, so as to minimise UK tax liabilities. This has far-reaching effects on the division of the tax pie between countries, their relative national incomes and so on. Although the imputation system in its standard forms does not suffer from the same drawback, it would do so if special concessions were embodied in it.[10]

To summarise the merits of alternative forms of corporation tax, we may say that domestically there are distinct differences between the separate and integrated systems in terms of equity, allocation of capital funds etc. From an international viewpoint, the integrated system may have disadvantages for capital flows even if all member countries have the same tax system; and if they do not, other more difficult problems arise.

Future Developments

The first question is whether there are supreme advantages in having a single corporation tax imposed at Community level instead of member-country taxes. It is far from clear that this is so. There is no overwhelming advantage in deriving Community revenue from this source rather than from VAT; in fact, the reverse might be the case. And despite the historical precedents of other federations, it would seem safer to predict that there is very little likelihood of any such development in the foreseeable future, even if it were intrinsically desirable.

The second question is whether the system of corporation tax needs to be, or could conceivably be, identical in all member countries. There are some arguments in favour of such a development. Governments would presumably have less trouble with such matters as arm's length pricing in that the temptation to switch the source of profits from one country to another would be less if, to quote a famous saying, 'there were no damned merit in it'. Companies would presumably also find it easier if the same company tax laws prevailed in all member countries. But one only needs to ask 'is it remotely conceivable?' to know the answer. The differences in definition of tax base, in concessions for depreciation or investment and in the extent of evasion are such that it seems quite out of the question that there could be anything like such an approximation of laws in the near future.

However, this does not mean that nothing should be done at all. There is a lot to be said for having the same corporation tax system in member countries. Liberalisation of capital flows is more likely to be achieved if all countries are on the same system, whether integrated or separate, than if they each go their own way. But having said that, we now come to the remaining question: should the common base be the separate system or the integrated one? As we have seen, the former has domestic disadvantages, but the latter has international ones. However, it would seem that the international disadvantages are less intractable than the domestic ones. If the imputation system prevailed in all member countries one could get over capital flow impediments by introducing a special credit for intra-EEC investment. Assume a British company invests in a subsidiary in France; if a special credit were allowed against French corporation tax, this would increase residual liability to British corporation tax and hence make it more likely that the payment of Advance Corporation Tax will not represent a *net* addition to tax liabilities. A device of this sort is a little cumbersome and might not eliminate all discrimination. But it could do so approximately, whereas there is no obvious means by which the domestic distortions due to the separate system could be avoided. So there is a very real justification for the EEC provisional decision in late 1973 to harmonise corporation taxes on the basis of the imputation system.

References

1. See G.S.A. Wheatcroft (ed.) *Value Added Tax in the Enlarged Common Market*, Cassell/Associated Business Programmes, London, 1973, for a recent account.

2. See R.A. Musgrave, *Fiscal Systems,* Yale University Press, 1969, for details.
3. Meaning the true rate, after allowing for evasion.
4. *Sixth Draft Directive* (on harmonisation of turnover taxes), EEC, Brussels, June 1973.
5. As is well-known, VAT (especially the origin type) has a close affinity to a payroll tax. Cf. C.S. Shoup, *Public Finance,* Aldine, Chicago, 1969, Chs. 9 and 16.
6. There are others such as the relative ease of varying personal income tax rates but not corporation tax (or vice-versa), counter-cyclical properties and so on; but we shall not explore them here.
7. The same arguments apply in the split rate case and so we shall not restate them in that context.
8. For the reason that Advance Corporation Tax has to be paid at the same time as, and to the same extent as, the credit given to shareholders when a dividend is declared. Whereas companies with domestic profits can offset such advance payments against their overall liability to UK Corporation tax, no such offsetting is possible when foreign, as distinct from British, corporation tax, is paid.
9. The problem should not be exaggerated. It is sometimes argued that the tax rate on an investor in country A should be the same as that on an investor in country B, assuming each invests in country C. This is a fallacy. The relevant criterion relates to one investor's return from each of two investments and not to each of two investors' returns from one investment.
10. See *infra,* p. 97.

7 DEVELOPMENT OF A EUROPEAN COMMUNITY BUDGET

Douglas Dosser

Background to a Federal Fiscal Structure

The present and prospective size of the Community budget, expressed as a proportion of Community GNP, is miniscule compared with the 30 per cent or so of GNPs channelled through the budgets of member states. Whether the Community budget grows to attain the stature of the federal budgets of the USA, Canada and Australia is an entirely open question today. Certainly, it is a far more daunting and difficult process than was the development of those federal fiscal systems.

For no division of powers and functions, with accompanying fiscal provisions, can be found in constitutional law or practice. The Treaty of Rome never made such provisions, and the Treaty of Accession included but a few fiscal clauses, embodying previous Summit agreements, of which the principal was the receipt of *ressources propres* by the Community from 1975 (1978 for the new members). On the expenditure side, no quantitative detail was entered into for the prospective regional, social and industrial policies; at the time of the enlargement, only the ongoing Common Agricultural Policy (CAP) implied a quantitive size for budget expenditures.

What quantification existed on the revenue and expenditure sides had arisen from *ad hoc* and usually crisis-ridden decisions. Compared with a treaty division of functions and the establishment of a federal budget at the outset, it is rather obvious that this piecemeal approach is going to continue. Since the Treaty of Accession, the financial specification of the regional policy is undergoing such treatment, and we shall no doubt see a continuation of the tortured process with the other prospective fields of policy, including a revamped CAP.

This is not the only difficulty, and difference, when comparing the European with the North American and Australian experiences. Those fiscal federations were set up in economies very different from the complex, industrialised, interdependent economies of the Community. This makes the European task much more difficult in many respects. For example, instead of developing a company law, or industrial subsidy schemes, or personal income tax systems *ab initio,* the disentangling of member states' codes and practices if a common system is desired can make it appear impossible.

Juxtaposed with complex economic systems, we have today a much greater complexity of instruments of economic policy, again in contrast with the period of establishment of other major fiscal federations. Not only have we to add the Keynsian instruments of expenditure and debt policies to traditional tax instruments, but also legislative prices and income policies, which have become so important in the last few years. A proper division of functions between levels of the fisc should include an appropriate division of all these fiscal, monetary and legislative instruments.

A great problem in considering this subject is whether the development of the Community budget should be studied as an extrapolation of the current, *ad hoc,* lop-sided approach, or an attempt made to see what makes economic sense in dividing economic tasks and instruments between the Community and member state public authorities in present-day Europe. The first makes more political sense, the latter more economic sense. We shall follow both paths, beginning with the more practical and realistic.

The Global Size of the Community Budget

The medium-term period, 1974-80, is divisible into two parts, the official second stage of economic and monetary union, 1974-76, and the further stage to the still-official target date for the fulfilment of the Werner plan in 1980.

There is a distinct difference between these two periods in looking at the growth of the Community budget; for we have an official target for its size in 1976,[1] and some substantive blue-prints for some of the revenue sources and expenditure components to that date. The second half, 1976-80, will be much more conjectural.

We can approach the growth of a budget either from the expenditure side, that is, the demand for public goods and services, or from the viewpoint that budgetary growth is usually tax-led, that is to say, opportunities arise, often from wars and crises, for the institutionalisation of new tax forms and sources, which permit the planning of new public expenditure programmes.

Demand for public services on a Community level

The proper way to proceed here is, of course, to consider particular possible public expenditure programmes one-by-one. But at the very best, we have to look at broad categories, such as 'regional policy', without much detailed information as to their precise content. Even with such broad categorisation, we cannot get very far. Estimates available for broad fields suggest this picture for 1976[2]

Policy Area	Expenditure in 1976 (million U.A.) (1973 prices)
CAP	5,250
Regional Fund	1,000
Social Fund	471 (1974)
Employment Fund	Not known
Industrial Policy	Not known

The figure for the CAP allows a little more than proportional growth, compared with an assumed real rate of growth of Community GNP of 4 per cent p.a., from about 0.5 per cent of Community GNP to 0.6 per cent. The figure for the Regional Fund in 1976 is the Commission's proposal, not agreed at the time of writing.

Not much progress can be made on the demand side in this way. Resort has to be made to broad extrapolation. The Community budget represented 0.57 per cent of Community GNP in 1973. A steady rate of growth to 1.0 per cent of Community GNP might look reasonable for 1976. This is, in fact, the standing official figure.

It does fit fairly well with the policy area approach. For 1.0 per cent of Community GNP in 1976 implies a resource use (at 1973 prices, with a 4.0 per cent p.a. real rate of growth) of approximately 8,750 million U.A., i.e. a balance after CAP of 3,500 million U.A., of which regional policy might take about a third.

When we come to the second part of the medium term, 1976-80, there is no basis for constituent expenditure policies and we have to rely solely on broad extrapolation. Elsewhere[3] alternative hypotheses of 2.0 per cent of Community GNP, and 3.0 per cent have been used. These yield the following figures (at 1973 prices, with a continued 4.0 per cent real rate of growth):

Policy Area	Expenditure in 1980 (million U.A.) (1973 prices)
CAP	6,200
Other	14,300 or 24,550
Total	20,500 or 30,750

The CAP estimate is on the same basis, 0.6 per cent of Community GNP; the balance is available for all other policies.

Financing Possibilities for the Community Budget

When we look at the implications of financing Community budgets equal to 1.0 per cent, 2.0 per cent or 3.0 per cent of Community GNP, we may find that they either encourage, just permit, or constrain these targets developed from the demand side.

The broad sources of finance are as follows:

(a) Common External Tariff and Agricultural Levies.

Under the *resources propres* agreements, the Community has the right to the proceeds from these from 1975 (1978 for the acceding members). It is estimated that they approximate to 0.5 per cent of Community GNP in 1973.

(b) VAT

If the base of the VAT is harmonised along the lines of the proposed Sixth Directive, raising revenues equal to 0.5 per cent of Community GNP requires approximately the imposition of a 1.0 per cent VAT rate around the Community.

(c) Corporation Tax

This alternative source of tax revenue has been suggested. If the Community were to receive the revenues from all existing corporation taxes, this would be equivalent to the yield of about a 3.25 per cent VAT rate.

(d) Debt Finance

The Community budget might be partly financed 'below the line' by the creation of long- or short-dated bonds. These might be issued by the new Community monetary authority in the new European currency unit.

(e) Money Creation

As a European currency unit gained in acceptability, initially having been issued against a backing of holdings of member-state currencies, a fiduciary issue might be possible, which would be used to finance in part a Community budgetary deficit.

The use of the personal income tax, excises and social security contributions have been left out of account. It is usually assumed that, at least in the medium term, income tax would remain entirely under the control of member states, in order to permit discretion in the global size of member-state budgets; and similarly for social security contributions. Excises would provide too narrow a base for the finance of the central budget of the federation.

From the available sources of finance, the agreed *resources propres* provision for the VAT (a yield of up to 1.0 per cent going to the Community) just provides the extra 0.5 per cent of Community GNP, which, added to Common External Tariff and levy revenues, finances the 1976 Community budget of 1.0 per cent of Community GNP.

Thus, there is a rough conformity between the 'demand' approach and the 'financing' approach to the 1976 budget. When we come to the broad extrapolation for 1980, no such conformity is visible; it is difficult to see how expenditure components or financing methods will develop. We will, however, examine these in more detail to see what picture can be built up for 1980.

Expenditure Components

Tendencies, propsects and problems of each existing or developing field of Community expenditure are looked at in turn.

(i) CAP

Since the accession of the new members pressure has been growing for a fundamental revision. This will almost certainly be an attempt at a new emphasis on the 'structural-efficiency' part of the programme at the expense of the 'income-support' section (which at present accounts for some 90 per cent of the funds). Whether the revisions will concern only the balance, or involve an actual reduction in the total of the programme, is an open question. However, even a shift implies a reduction in size in the long run, since improvements in the productive efficiency of Community agriculture narrow the gap between costs in the Community and outside and reduce the need for 'income support' through maintained prices. Thus the figure for CAP to 1980 of O.6 per cent of Community GNP may well be a considerable overestimate.

Current developments in world commodity prices, their fast rate of increase outside the Community, favour the same interpretation.

In consequence, a much larger balance may be available in the 1980 budget for other policies, though as we shall see, the agricultural developments noted above also act against one of the (agreed) sources of finance, the agricultural levies.

(ii) Regional Fund

The size of the Fund for the three year period, 1974-76, has been the subject of great dispute, with contention lying between a figure of £1,250 million and £250 million for the three years. Assuming a compromise is reached, it is clear that only a small figure, and only a third of the 'balance', is likely for 1976. A very much bigger 'balance' is implied for 1980, especially if the possible decline in CAP expenditure is allowed for. What prospects are there for a much larger Regional Fund in 1977-80 to take up this balance?

The prospects for a greatly increased Fund do not seem strong.[4] There is a likelihood of both growing ambiguity about the regional problem (whether all kinds of casualties of social and economic change, such as urban centres, should not have a claim) and growing disenchantment about financial subsidisation through the Community budget. In any case, it is disputed whether the conventional regional problem, as currently defined, will get worse or be moderated by increased factor mobility.

Both the immediate wrangles and the longer-term problems would seem to diminish the prospect of a Regional Fund being a substantial Community programme in 1980, especially in view of the overlap we shall observe between it and other prospective policies.[5]

(iii) Social Policy

The three areas of social policy are: the Social Fund (and new Employment Fund), social security harmonisation, and 'social innovation'.[6]

A small increase in the Social Fund is officially envisaged for 1974. The argument exists that the more successfully the aims of EMU are achieved, which includes a faster real rate of growth of Community GNP, the more rapid the rate of industrial transformation, and the social cost of a higher rate of redundancy. Calculations of this rate, and the cost of dealing with it along the lines of standards recommended by the OECD, show that the cost per annum could rise to £7,000 million if redundancy rose to 3¾ million per annum.[7] A good deal of the 'balance' of the Community budget could therefore be taken up in the later 1970s by Social Fund policy. It could be justified on the grounds of diverting some of the increased real income accruing to the gainers from EMU to the losers, and would partly supplant the Regional Fund, removing the specifically geographical aspect from that policy.

Social security harmonisation could involve vast increases in public expenditure, as has been pointed out, if Community norms were established at levels of 'best provision' in each field: unemployment and redundancy pay, industrial injury compensation, family and maternity allowances, pensions, low-income supplementation, health and educational services. The prospects whether such upward alignment would be approached in the medium term must vary from one area of policy to another; there is also some uncertainty whether such upward harmonisation need necessarily require to be financed through the Community budget.

On looking more closely at the list, the prime candidate for action would appear to be unemployment and other employment-related payments. There is already a plan to put this partly on a Community basis in the new Employment Fund as well as in the Social Fund (and Regional Fund). The OECD levels used in the calculations referred to do not reach the best Community (German) levels. But the process is in train, and it was implied earlier that it would at least partly go through the Community budget, and be tax-financed.

Most of the other fields of social security are firmly embedded in member-state budgets, and are financed by a varying mix of employer-employee-general tax finance. No medium-term policies under discussion for the Community involve them. For example, family allowances and low-income supplementation are embedded in the income tax system, and lie right outside the discussion of harmonisation at present; as do health provision and educational systems and standards. Thus there is not much scope for Community budgetary expansion in the social security field, other than that which is employment-related.

The Community's social policy document mentions several other possible developments: special employment policies for women, youth, and minority groups; improving the quality of work in manufacturing industry, worker participation in industry, etc. Most of these are unquantified, unquantifiable, and in any case, would appear to impinge financially on the private sector rather than the public. This does not seem an area for substantial Community budgetary operation, although it might be for Community standards and regulations.

(iv) Industrial Policy

The Community industrial policy document[8] does of course involve vast potential Community expenditures. The Community is supposed to promote scale and reorganisation. There may be general assistance for small firms, especially in new technology areas, or subsidisation of vast sectoral projects. The great example, the Concorde aircraft, though not a fully Community project, shows how expensive such ventures can be. But it is an entirely open question at present whether either general programmes, or sectoral projects, are going to get off the ground at all, and it is hardly likely during the medium term under discussion.

(v) Other Expenditure Policies

There are faltering attempts to develop an energy policy, but more as a joint negotiating position on oil than one involving public expenditures. On the other hand, energy supply systems involving transfrontier grids would offer as yet undefined scope for Community operation. Transport policy would appear to offer scope for the Community budget to finance both motorway and rail systems, though the main item at present, the Channel Tunnel, is again a bilateral rather than a Community enterprise.

It has to be concluded that it is difficult to see on what policies the 'balance' of funds in 1980 is to be expended. CAP expenditure should decline, regional policy looks a poor card, industrial, energy and transport policies are quite undeveloped in concept and principle; only Social Fund expenditure on unemployment, redundancy and retraining appears to be a strong force. The view cannot be avoided, after the discussion in this section, that the Community budget will look as lop-sided as now in comparison with member-state budgets; an income-support and structural-support policy for ailing manufacturing will be added to, or partly substituted for, the similar programme which now exists for agriculture; and perhaps with a similar bias towards income subsidy rather than the promotion of increased efficiency.

Budgetary Finance

As we saw earlier, three groups of sources of finance are conceivable: tariffs and import levies, taxes, and monetary policies.

(i) Tariffs and Levies

The global figures we wrote in for these sources in 1980, namely, revenue equivalent to 0.5 per cent of Community GNP, is probably an overestimate. True, we can look forward to trade expansion, but mainly inside the Community, and with some trade diversion from outside. The granting of associate membership, and the negotiation of trade pacts with more and more countries militates against this source of revenue. Again, new mutual tariff-cutting involving the USA may be in store. These processes may be accelerated by the presence of the UK.

The agricultural levies may also prove an undynamic source of revenue, for the very reasons for which we expected a decline in CAP expenditure: the closing of the gap between world and Community commodity price levels.

These twin sources of finance reserved for the Community in the Council Resolutions of 1970 and 1971, and in the Treaty of Accession, are also the very ones that are the cause of the over-proportional (to GNP) gross payments of the UK to the Community, and will continue to be most under attack by the UK.

(ii) Tax Finance

The desirability of the VAT as the main general sales tax in member states, harmonised to a greater or lesser degree, has to be judged on several other criteria, rather than just as a source of revenue for the Community budget.[9] But here we concentrate on this aspect.

The VAT, which is already envisaged officially as the major Community means of tax finance, has some obvious advantages. If the base is harmonised along the lines of the proposed Sixth Directive, it is near to being a proportional levy on member states, proportional to consumption per head, and to GNP per head, in so far as the consumption/GNP ratio is roughly the same in each state.[10] This removes some of the objection by the UK to current financial plans. Further, it is a tax with a lot of leverage, for as we have seen, only a 1.0 per cent VAT rate transfers 0.5 per cent of the Community GNP to the public sector.

If the VAT is the best prospect for Community financing, the big problem is how the Community rate is going to be increased from the currently agreed 1 per cent for 1976 (indeed, how that is to be activated in some countries) to the 3 per cent to 5 per cent we have envisaged in working hypotheses on global size for 1980.

The simplest way would be the maintenance of existing levels of rates in the member states, and the reduction of revenue receipts by member states as increasing percentage points were paid over to meet the Community's requirements. There are two objections to this. The Commission itself still aims for a near-equalisation of (total) rates in member states; and also member states are hardly likely to cut their own revenues (and expenditures?) at such a significant rate by 1980.

However, anything less than complete submission on these two points by the Community or the member states involves us in a new, and very modern problem. An increase in the overall rate (in UK and Germany by virtue of harmonising to a norm of 15 to 17 per cent in all member states, if the Community rate is to be piled on top of the national rate) is hardly conceivable at present, because of the indirect tax/wage spiral, unless it is intended to neutralise the new revenues in budget surpluses or reductions in deficits.

A way out of this impasse is the concept of a 'shadow' system of Community taxation. The Community would receive the revenue-equivalent of a 1 per cent or 2 per cent VAT on the harmonised Community base from a member state, but that state would have discretion over how it actually raised that revenue. There are various degrees of 'shadowing' reality. The state might actually have to raise the funds from VAT, but could apply a zero rate to some sectors, such as food (which would be implicitly taxed at the Community rate) while making up the revenue requirement for the Community by an increased rate on other sectors. Or, going much further, the member state might raise its contribution to the Community from an entirely different tax source, the percentage of a VAT base becoming only a formula to calculate its contribution. As one moves beyond the short step away from a real Community system implied by zero-rating of food (which may still be politically necessary for the UK in 1978) shadow systems become, of course, less and less satisfactory from the Community's point of view, because they represent a return to member state direct contributions, which it was the whole purpose of the *ressources propres* agreements to replace.

While the VAT still represents the best medium-term prospect for financing the Community budget, its use bristles with problems which are, at the time of writing, quite unresolved.

The only other tax candidate is the corporation tax. This might form a source of Community finance in the longer run. In the medium term, however, the difficulties of harmonising the base for a uniform application of a Community rate appear insurmountable. Further, its use would require more sophisticated views about the equity of member-state contributions than the simple near-proportionality of the VAT. It might eventually be argued that those countries with the highest level of incorporated business (indicating industrial advancement in some sense) should pay most; or that if larger and possibly transnational companies will be the chief gainers from some of the Community's policies, for example its industrial policy, they should pay according to the benefit principle. Indeed, this last remark indicates what might be the solution for the use of the corporation tax for Community revenues, namely that a Community corporation tax be developed along with the proposed Community company code, and firms incorporating under the latter would pay tax direct to the Community. The problem to solve would be the inter-relationship with member state corporation taxes. But the proposal would partially satisfy the benefit principle, and have useful political advantages in putting the tax charge where opinion was not so averse to taxes for the Community, and not so provocative to wage-bargainers, as extra VAT would be.

(iii) Money and Credit

The possibility of a shortfall of tax revenues for the expenditures of the Community gives rise to the highly contentious issue of Community money creation, if and when a European currency unit comes into existence. This last qualification makes this an unlikely source of revenue in the medium term, although monetary union is still a declared aim for 1980. Moreover, strong opinion exists against any further expansion of liquidity, especially in the light of the Community's own declared counter-inflation policy. But it has been counter-argued that the new European currency would aim to replace (uncontrolled) Eurodollar liquidity.[11]

The other non-tax means is, of course, debt-creation on the part of the European monetary authorities. The technical problems of this are, of course, dealt with elsewhere in this volume,[12] and it is clear that, in view of the complexity of co-ordination with member-state debt policies, there is little prospect of finance on any sizeable scale by this method in the medium term. In any case, money and debt creation could only credibly finance a small part of expenditures, the latter themselves giving rise to new expenditures (of interest payments) which would involve at least part tax finance if credibility and confidence in the European currency were to be upheld.

The Community Budget in the Longer Term

Our discussion of the medium term has not given rise to very bright prospects for the steady development of a Community budget. There is a lack of rational and balanced expenditure programmes, beyond agriculture, and serious problems about financing them, even if they existed. It is a matter of some doubt whether progress towards a federal budgetary structure, to match political and business trends in Europe, is going to be achieved by the halting, *ad hoc,* unbalanced progress so far experienced on both the expenditure and financing sides. A better approach altogether might be to seek a division of budgetary powers founded on principle, at least as a guide to desirable (versus undesirable) partial moves in that direction. This procedure would also help to justify the development of a Community budget, whereas present procedures only confirm the sceptics' view of it as a hotch-potch of ephemeral programmes. Certainly, indications can be given of a proper division of fiscal functions among public authorities in the new Europe, as it is developing as a result of trade and business integration.

Such an indication can be briefly given under the three standard budgetary heads as follows:

(i) Allocation of Resources

In each member state, the public sector now controls upwards of 30 per cent of the GDP directly, and exerts influence to a greater or lesser degree over the allocation of resources in much of the private sector. Dealing with the public sector's own supply of goods and services, and using the distinction between 'social' goods and 'merit' goods, there is an economic argument for Community provision, as contrasted with member-state provision, in the following cases:

(a)   The impossibility of excluding people from the benefits of the provision of some good or service has recently been a prime argument for justifying its provision by a public authority. Non-exclusibility arises from technical characteristics of the good; if it is provided at all, a minimum coverage is inevitable. The best application for the Community would be defence, if it were not for the particular historic situation which exists in Europe. Modern nuclear defence implies large-scale public provision, which is recognised by the existence of NATO. Some international policing services could legitimately also be Community-financed, where they are aimed against international crime, for example drug-running.

An alternative case for public provision of social goods exists where technical considerations imply non-exclusibility, but the area can be chosen on least-cost criteria. This is a much richer field for Community operation. Applications can be seen in law and order services, and transport and energy policies, especially where grid systems are required.

Further, where the provision of social goods is rationalised under the non-exclusibility criterion, the Community has a role in solving the 'tapering-off' problem. The benefit area concept, as used above, is less distinct than implied. The benefits of law and order services, pollution control, etc., spill over to varying extents to adjoining areas under different jurisdiction. Indeed, the areas of jurisdiction may be immutable and spill over common and inevitable. The federal authority then has the role of arranging compensatory payments, or a transfer system (quite apart from any redistributory transfer systems).

(b) Merit goods are in a different category and would depend for Community provision on the growth of 'common feeling' across the Community which would require provision of a good or service by the Community on a different scale from that which would ensue from individuals acting in the market. Eventually, such a situation might arise in health and education, (provision of minimum levels or standards for all) though it is obviously still a long way off.

Increasing technical progress and associated social integration through increased travel and communication is likely to increase the range of goods and services which might justifiably be provided at Community level, both in the social and merit categories.

(ii) Stabilisation Policy

Considerable discussion is taking place on the degree of need for the operation of monetary and fiscal instruments for stabilisation policy on a Community level. The matter will therefore only be briefly dealt with here.[13]

There is a political or administrative time-span to this problem, and an economic one. The political one is the rate at which member-state instruments of economic management are going to be vitiated by decisions about monetary and tax arrangements, usually taken on grounds other than stabilisation: for example, revenues for Community provision of goods and services, tax harmonisation for equalisation of business conditions, or simply political consolidation of the Community *vis-a-vis* the outside world. This may apply to member-state exchange rate policy, budget surplus/deficit positions, bank credit and hire purchase policy, and VAT variation.

This is an untidy approach, especially in the context of this section, where some reference to economic principles for the determination of the role of the Community budget is intended. The crucial questions in the economic approach are: what is the rate of consolidation of member-state variations in aggregate demand around some trends (of given combination of inflation and unemployment), and which are the best instruments to give the Community to deal with the consolidated cycle?

The consolidation itself is dependent on various trends.[14] There is considerable lack of knowledge, and much dispute, as to the degree to which consolidation is at present occurring. The issue will not be entered into here, but any substantiation of it would provide a justification for either action directly by the Community or the co-ordination of member-state action by the Community. Otherwise, autonomous member-state action would be to a degree either non-effective or inconvenient and embarrassing for other member states.

Assuming consolidation and therefore the need for Community policy, the question still arises as to the instruments it should use. The whole Community economy can, of course, be adjusted *vis-a-vis* the outside, by use of the Community exchange rate. But usually an internal policy of reflation/deflation would be followed also. This could be operated by internal monetary and credit policies, by variation in Community tax rates (VAT) or by commanded variations in taxes remaining within the ambit of member states.

We cannot go into these issues in detail here. The relevant and key point is the prospect that the European budget will necessarily have a stabilisation role to play in future years. The only possible alternative is that, while monetary instruments, which are not budgetary instruments, necessarily pass to the Community, fiscal policy for stabilisation should be left with member states but under Community control. The national budgets really then become agents for the Community in this function, and those parts of member-state budgets implicitly add up to a Community budget.

(iii) Redistribution of Income

The above policies of the Community budget have redistributional side-effects but here we deal with the intended redistributional role. An attempt has been made elsewhere to apply a number of the standard variations of federal redistributive policy to the Community.[15]

The first distinction is, of course, between federal solutions and centralisation involving direct fiscal relationships between the Community and its citizens. The various federal solutions; transfer systems to equalise money or real expenditures per head in given fields of public provision, to equalise fiscal potential, or matching grants to upgrade public provision in given fields: must all founder so long as the principle of *juste retour* is insisted upon by member states. Of course, a breach of this principle is implied under the preceding two heads of budgetary policy, for it would be both irrational and extremely difficult to assign the 'benefits' of the Community provision of public goods, and operation of stabilisation policy, to individual member states. But, on the contrary, it is easy to identify benefits to member states of transfers, and it seems likely that *juste retour* will be hung on to in this branch of the budget after it has been necessarily abandoned in the other two branches.

Of course, there is an element of income redistribution in the agricultural and regional policies, of the nature of matching grants (since the programmes are on top of member states subsidisation of the agricultural sector and depressed regions). But here the argument currently rages, on the basis of *juste retour,* of the two programmes taken in conjunction, thus preventing an overall redistributive effect between states. In any case, we have earlier thought relatively little of the long-run prospects of these policies.

Direct redistributive relationships between the Community budget and Community citizens could come with direct elections to the European Parliament and development of European political parties; this development obviously has a very long time horizon. The prospect for an active redistributive role on the part of the Community budget seems much lower (or has a much longer time horizon) than public goods provision and stabilisation policy. The reason may be simply this. Increasing scale (involving productive methods, communications, business organisation) is demanding Community operations of the first two kinds, but the same factors do not apply to policies for the redistribution of income, which depend more on moral, ethical or community feeling, to which the scale argument does not apply.

Conclusion

Our discussion of the medium-term prospects and the longer-term rationale for a Community or federal budget leads to a paradox. Present tendencies in the Community budget do not seem very dynamic on the revenue side, considering the CET and Agricultural Levies and increases in VAT rates; on the expenditure side, we have only the disputed agricultural and regional policies, and the non-specified social and industrial policies. There is a feeling of *malaise,* and it would seem difficult to get towards the 2 to 3 per cent of Community GNP level.

On the other hand, the ultimate role of the Community budget in the context of developing business and technical Europe, must be a substantial one; some have attached the figure of 10 per cent of Community GNP to it.[16]

So long as the Community budget and its financing is added to existing member-state programmes only fragmentary progress will be made towards a federal budget, which ought rationally to take over some of the budgetary programmes of member states. The gap between the way things are going and where they ought rationally to arrive is a stark one. How the political process will develop it is difficult to see at present. The key must be the transfer of political sovereignty to match the steadily growing autonomous economic integration.

References

1. See EEC, *Communication from the Commission to the Council on the First and Second Stages of EMU*, COM(73) 570, Brussels, April 1973.
2. Figures from D. Dosser and J. Pinder, *European Economic Union*, Croom Helm, for Federal Trust, London, 1974.
3. Figures from D. Dosser and J. Pinder, *Economic Union in the EEC*, Croom Helm, for Federal Trust, London, 1974.
4. See Chapter 5.
5. For contrast between the more optimistic and more critical approaches, compare the Commission's documents COM(73) 550, May 1973, COM (73) 1170, July 1973; COM(73) 1171, July 1973; COM(73) 1218, July 1973; COM(73) 1751, Oct 1973; with the Dosser-Pinder Report, op.cit.
6. See EEC, *Guidelines for a Social Programme*, COM(73) 528, April 1973.
7. Worked out in detail in Dosser and Pinder, op.cit., section III.3.
8. EEC, *Memorandum on the Technological and Industrial Policy Programme*, SEC(73) 1090, 3 May 73.
9. See the discussion of VAT in Chapter 6 pp. 90-95 above.
10. Of course, this remark does not apply to the *net* payments/receipts of a state from the Community budget.
11. The contribution that money creation might make to the European budget is calculated in EEC, *European Economic Integration and Monetary Unification*, Brussels, October 1973, Section III, E.3. Also the arguments for and against European liquidity creation are displayed in the appendix papers of G. Magnifico, R.A. Mundell, and W. Neubauer.
12. See Chapter 3.
13. See also Chapter 2 above.
14. Five are listed in a recent OECD Report: price effects, demand effects from exports, liquidity effects, multinational corporation and trade union links. See OECD, *Economic Outlook*, No. 13, Paris 1973.
15. See D. Dosser, 'Notes on Some Public Finance Issues as they Relate to Economic Union', in EEC, *European Economic Integration and Monetary Unification*, Brussels, October 1973.
16. For example, Steven Robson in Chapter 2, p. 20 above.

NOTES ON CONTRIBUTORS

Geoffrey Denton is a Reader in Economics at the University of Reading, and Research Director at the Federal Trust

Douglas Dosser is Professor of Economic Theory at the University of York

Santosh Mukherjee is a Research Officer at the Institute of Statistics, University of Oxford

Alan Prest is Professor of Economics at the London School of Economics

Adam Ridley* was an Economic Adviser in the Central Policy Review Staff, Cabinet Office, and is now on the panel of advisors to H.M. Leader of the Opposition

Steven Robson* is an Economic Adviser in the Treasury

Paul Woolley is a Research Fellow in the Department of Economic and Social Research, University of York

* Although employed in an official capacity at the time these papers were written, Mr. Ridley and Mr. Robson wish to make clear that their contributions represent only their own personal views and not official policy.

INDEX

117

For Product Safety Concerns and Information please contact our EU representative GPSR@taylorandfrancis.com Taylor & Francis Verlag GmbH, Kaufingerstraße 24, 80331 München, Germany

Printed and bound by CPI Group (UK) Ltd, Croydon, CR0 4YY

08/05/2025

01864412-0001